# Preface

As an NRI, investing in Mutual Funds can often feel complex, due to added regulations and an investing structure that may seem foreign to many living outside of India. Making the right choice as an investment may seem challenging and that's the reason I wrote this book. To illustrate the complete process in a simple manner to help you make your investment decisions with complete confidence.

In this book, I've gathered years of research and experience to provide practical insights that cater specifically to NRI investors. From the basics to more advanced strategies, this guide is meant to equip you with the tools to grow your wealth and build a lasting financial legacy for your family.

Whether you're an experienced investor or just starting out, I hope this book serves as an available resource for you. To help you reach your financial goals effectively. Let's work together to unlock the potential of mutual funds and create wealth that stands the test of time.

**Jugal Baldawa**

# Table of Content

Chapter 1 – Why India? A Land of Opportunities for the NRIs

Chapter 2 – How NRIs Can Invest in India via Mutual Funds

Chapter 3 – First Step: Open Up an NRE Account

Chapter 4 – Why Mutual Funds and Regular SIPs in Mutual Funds

Chapter 5 – Navigating the Rules: SEBI and Investor Protection for NRI

Chapter 6 – How to Invest While Living Abroad: A Look at Some Smart Strategies

Chapter 7 – Protecting Your Wealth by Diversifying Beyond Mutual Funds

Chapter 8 – Tax Talk: Smooth Sail through Indian and Foreign Taxation as an NRI

Chapter 9 – Tapping into the Future of India's Emerging Sectors

Chapter 10 – A Guide to Retirement and Investment Options

Chapter 11 - Creating Wealth that Lasts for Generations to Come

Chapter 12 - Success Stories of the NRI Investors

The Conclusion

# Chapter 1

# Why India? A Land of Opportunities for the NRIs

As of 2024, the Indian Stock Market ranks 4th in the entire world in terms of total market capitalisation. Indian population's median age is just 28 years old, hence, India has one of the youngest populations in the world. With a GDP growth rate higher than any other major economy, its stock market is poised for serious growth.

But what does it mean for an average NRI and what makes it the golden pot for them to lay their hands on?

Before we look into the essentials of investing in the Indian stock market, let's just understand some basic facts about the Indian Stock Market. How it came into existence and what makes it special, especially for the diverse group of NRIs out there.

- Indian Stock Market is the first of its kind in Asia. It's run by two prominent exchanges, NSE (National Stock Exchange) and BSE (Bombay Stock Exchange)

- Bombay Stock Exchange was established in 1875 as the first stock exchange in Asia.

- NSE was founded in 1992 and is the biggest stock exchange in India in terms of total volume.

- The two prominent Indian Market Indexes are Sensex and NIFTY 50 (similar to Dow Jones and NASDAQ in the U.S.).

- The Indian Stock Market is regulated by SEBI (Securities and Exchange Board of India)

Now that we know the basics of the Indian stock market. Let's understand what makes it special for the NRIs.

## 1. Highest Number of Listed Companies

Indian Stock Exchanges (NSE & BSE) boasts of the highest number of listed companies in the world. With 7575 companies listed in BSE and NSE by Jan 2024. This achievement makes it the world's biggest stock market in terms of listed companies. As of 2024, the Indian Stock Market is also the 4th biggest Stock market in the world in terms of Market Capitalisation.

## 2. Biggest Growth Rate

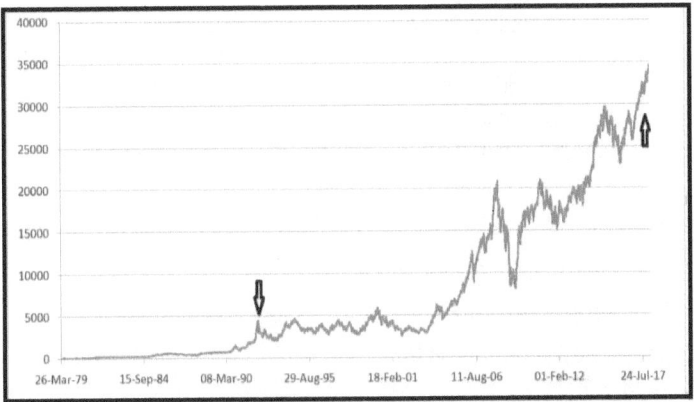

50 years on and the chart line only goes up

Since the past 30 years, Indian Stock Market has yielded an average return of 17%. Which is amongst the highest returns among all major economies in the world. Comparing it to the United States's 'S&P 500' which has yielded an average of about 10% returns annually.

## 3. Fastest Growing Economy

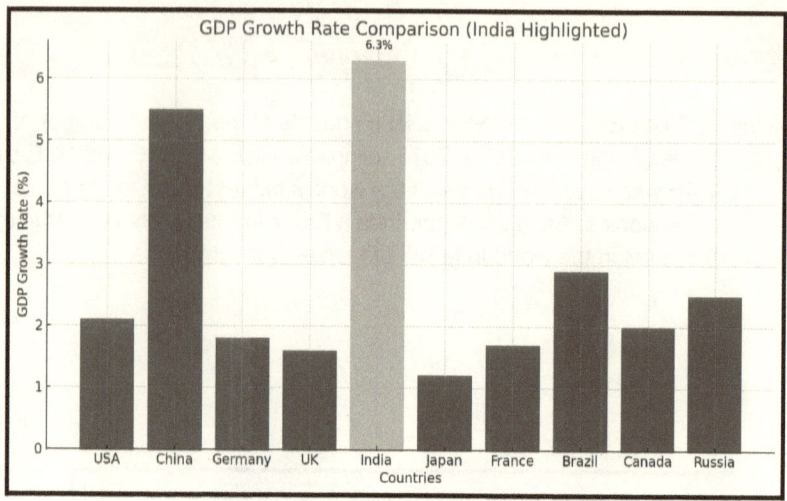

India has been the world's fastest growing major economy for almost a decade now. With an average growth rate of 7% annually, it's headed to the 3rd largest economy status by the end of 2030. And as we all know, GDP growth only comes with growth in products and services.
Which can only mean 1 thing for the country's stock market, a super steady rise.

Not to forget it has one of the youngest populations on earth, with a median age of just 28. This means that there are over 600 million people in a population of 1.4 Billion who are below the age of 28 and are yet to contribute to the country's growing economic success as a whole.

Perhaps the biggest reason for anyone who can, to invest in India.

## 4. The Rise of Mutual Funds

Mutual funds pool money from various investors to invest in a diversified portfolio of stocks, bonds, or other securities, which is managed by professional fund managers. And for NRIs mutual funds present an ideal solution, especially for those who may not have the time or expertise to invest directly in the stock market.

Since Mutual funds are a mixture of securities, so if the stock market is on the rise, it's safe to say that the mutual funds here will rise with it. And most of the time exceeding the stock market's returns rate.

For eg. The best performing equity mutual funds can offer outstanding returns of 30-40% annually. Which is more than twice the returns of the Stock market as a whole.

## MUTUAL FUNDS THAT HAVE GIVEN MORE THAN 45-65% RETURN IN 3 YEARS

| Funds | 3 Yr | 5 Yr | 10 Yr |
|---|---|---|---|
| Quant Small Cap Fund - Direct Plan | 65.59 | 25.73 | 16.33 |
| Quant Infrastructure Fund - Direct Plan | 53.34 | 22.59 | 19.15 |
| Nippon India Small Cap Fund - Direct Plan | 50.37 | 19.17 | 27.84 |
| Tata Small Cap Fund - Direct Plan | 47.15 | -- | -- |
| Canara Robeco Small Cap Fund - Direct Plan | 46.74 | -- | -- |
| Kotak Small Cap Fund - Direct Plan | 46.66 | 18.52 | 21.74 |
| Bandhan Sterling Value Fund - Direct Plan | 45.44 | 13.53 | 18.31 |
| Quant Tax Plan - Direct Plan | 45.15 | 23.83 | 23.04 |
| ICICI Prudential Infrastructure Fund - Direct Plan | 44.52 | 16.63 | 16.24 |
| SBI Contra Fund - Direct Plan | 44.45 | 17.25 | 16.07 |

Data as on 31st May 2023; Source: Value Research

Analytics by Business Today

Now who wouldn't want to invest in such an economy in their right mind? Well, the right answer is 'none', as in no one in their right mind would wanna miss this golden opportunity. This is not far from the truth as there's no major corporation in the world that hasn't invested in the Indian stock market.

## What are the Reasons Behind Such Remarkable Growth and How Long Can It Last?

India hasn't stuck oil like the middle east. Well there is some oil but it isn't even enough for its own consumption, let alone for the exports to drive its growth. Its economic success journey hasn't been an overnight triumph. It's a result of several key economic reforms that have been implemented over the years to strengthen and safeguard its economy.

Ever since India attained a liberalised economy status back in 1991, the government has consistently introduced policies that are aimed at promoting growth and attracting FDI (foreign direct investment).

But what do such policies look like and what makes them highly regarded? Let's have a look at some of them.

- **Goods and Services Tax (GST)**: The Indian tax system used to be composed of some complex tax methods but with the introduction of GST, the Indian tax system has been simplified for the average citizen.
  This has further led to a positive impact on sectors such as manufacturing and services, which in turn has benefitted the growth of the stock market.

- **Make in India Initiative**: This has been one of the most crucial initiatives in boosting the manufacturing sector and attracting foreign companies to set up their operations in India.
  For NRIs, this translates into investment opportunities in sectors that are poised for exponential growth.

- **Digital India Drive**: India's digital transformation has been one of the biggest game changers for its economy. With the world's second-largest internet user base, sectors such as e-commerce, fintech, and digital services are booming.
  For NRIs, this means that they can tap into this growth through mutual funds focused on technology and innovation.

- **Banking and Financial Reforms**: With digitalisation comes the growing penetration of digital banking. And the government has left no stone unturned to contribute to this change. They have amended policy to give financial institutions a push which has led to remarkable growth in the Indian financial services sector over the years.
  Mutual funds focusing on banking and financial services are now among the top-performing funds in the market.

Hence, as you can see it hasn't been an overnight success story that can change in the blink of an eye. It has been a result of years of reforms and research, and as we all know more the effort one lays down into building something, the harder it is for it to fail. Which has been the front cover story of the Indian financial market for decades.

# Where the Biggest Growth in the Indian Market Lies for the NRIs?

The biggest growth as usual lies in the trends of technological advancements where India has the upper hand to lead worldwide. As investing in a market is based on the assumption of the industry's future growth. So naturally, there are some industries that take the lead here. Below are some of these sectors:

- **Technology:** When it comes to the world of IT, India has been renowned for its highly regarded services. Mutual funds associated with this sector are assured to provide high returns in the future.

- **Financial Services:** The expansion of India's banking sector, along with the rise of the fintech industry, makes financial services a lucrative sector for long-term investment.

- **Healthcare:** In 2024, India stands as the country leading in medical tourism. All been made possible by its cost effective treatments and the availability of highly skilled Doctors.
NRIs should look for Mutual funds that invest in pharmaceutical and healthcare companies as these present an attractive opportunity for them to grow their wealth.

- **Infrastructure:** As the economy thrives, the very first thing it needs is a robust infrastructure to sustain its elevated services and consumption. So naturally, the Mutual funds that invest in industries dealing with infrastructure projects pose a great investment opportunity.

India happens to simply be the best investment opportunity for the NRIs. A land which truly is an unparalleled investment hub due to its combination of a fast-growing economy, a young and dynamic population, strong regulatory frameworks, and sectoral growth drivers are some of the reasons which make India a land of immense potential.

Even though NRIs are among the have-been citizens of India who have left it for greater opportunities. Now the scenario has changed, India has massive untapped potential and it has provided them with a way to reconnect with their roots and gain the benefit of its economic success being afar.

Investing in mutual funds in India allows NRIs to not only participate in the country's growth but also diversify their global portfolios in a way that is both financially rewarding and highly secure.

---∞---

# Chapter 2

# How NRIs Can Invest in India via Mutual Funds

In Chapter 1, we discussed the grand investment hub that is India, in the present scenario. And how NRIs like yourselves, who aren't exactly the citizens of the country, can still seek advantage of its growing economy and have the opportunity to create generational wealth for your future generations to come.

Now, as we move forward, here we will discuss all the ways that can help you as an NRI to invest your hard earned money safely into the Golden Pot of the 21st century.

## Glossary:

Before we begin with our bit of breaking down some complex terms for you. Here are the meanings of a few financial terms that we'll use in our current chapter. So you won't have to put down the book and rush to Google to check out the meanings of these terms.

- **PIS** - Potential Investment Scheme
- **NRO** - Non Resident Ordinary
- **NRE** - Non Resident External
- **FD** - Fixed Deposit
- **TDS** - Tax Deducted at Source
- **RBI** - Reserve Bank of India

## Breakdown of Complex Ways to Invest in Mutual Funds as an NRI

Now, as an Indian one typically needs a Demat account which any bank in India can set up for you. But for an NRI there are 2 options to choose from before they could begin their investing journey in India. An NRE and an NRO account. Here NRE stands for Non Resident External and NRO means Non Resident Ordinary Account.

Now let's get to know the major differences between the two from the table:

| NRE | NRO |
|---|---|
| 1. This Account can be used for depositing foreign currency only. | This account holds both your foreign money which you'll use to invest in Indian market and the INR (Indian Rupees). |
| 2. One can only deposit foreign currency in this type of account | One can Deposit both Indian and Foreign currency in this type of account. |
| 3. Typically used by NRIs who have no income or affiliation from India. | Typically used by NRIs who have other sources of income from India such as from rentals, FDs, freelance etc. |
| 4. An Account Holder can only be an NRI. | An Account Holder can be an NRI or an Indian Citizen. |
| 5. Interest Income earned from mutual funds is Tax-Free. | Interest Income earned from mutual funds is taxable. |
| 6. Funds can be transferred from NRE to NRO. | Funds cannot be transferred to an NRE account from this type of account. |

These are some of the differences between the two. Let's elaborate on the differences for a better and clearer understanding of the two.

## NRE

- This type of account is suited best for people who are totally unaligned from their ancestral country, India. Those who have no family, or any sort of investment such as real estate, other businesses etc. usually prefer to choose this account.

## NRO

☐ This type of account is chosen by those who have a family as citizens of India and have certain types of investments in the country. In short, a person who is very well associated with India despite living and earning in a foreign country.

As we've discussed these two bank accounts that NRIs need in order to receive and deposit money into their trading/demat accounts. Now let's get to know the types of trading/demat accounts NRIs need to invest in mutual funds. These are of two types: PIS and Non PIS. Here, PIS stands for 'Portfolio Investment Scheme', hence, you get the meaning of the latter.

Now let's find out the difference between these two trading/demat accounts.

| PIS | Non PIS |
|---|---|
| 1. Under this scheme one can invest in Mutual Funds through both NRE and NRO bank accounts. | Under this scheme, one can only invest in Mutual funds using NRO accounts. |
| 2. Only certain banks accept NRE and NRO banks through this scheme. The banks are: HDFC, Indusind, IDFC First, Axis and Yes Bank. | NRO accounts under this scheme can be with any bank. There are no restrictions to choose from any particular one in general. |
| 3. Under PIS, a permission letter has to be obtained from the RBI via your partner bank. | In Non PIS, you don't need a letter from RBI to begin your investor's journey. |
| 4. Here, the funds from the bank account have to be transferred to the PIS first. The bank then conveys this information to your trading broker after which the funds become available in your trading account. The entire process can take up to a day. | Here, the funds for investing are transferred from the NRO account instantly to the trading account using net banking. |

| | |
|---|---|
| 5. In PIS, the bank deducts and pays TDS on short term capital gains which is 20% and long term capital gains (12.5% above 1,25,000/year). | In Non PIS, your broker handles TDS on the account. There are no additional charges for collecting and reporting TDS. |
| 6. BTST (Buy today sell tomorrow) is not available | BTST is available in Non PIS Accounts. |
| 7. Brokerage is 0.5% or 200 INR per order, whichever is lower. | Brokerage is 0.5% or 100 INR per executed order, whichever is lower. |
| 8. One can repatriate the entire amount | One can only repatriate the interest earned on your investment. |

As an NRI you can choose to open NRO-NON PIS Account, an NRO-PIS or an NRE-PIS Account. This means that the person with an NRO account has the option of choosing both PIS and Non PIS trading accounts but an NRE bank account holder only has the option of choosing a PIS account which is a relatively comfortable option for an NRI with no affiliation with India.

Especially due to the reason that one can repatriate (the act or process of returning or restoring something to the country of origin, or citizenship) the entire amount invested. Which isn't possible with an NRO, PIS Account. As under these one can

So, this was all you needed to know about both the types of trading accounts, PIS and Non PIS. In case you think you missed a detail or two, flip the page back and have a look at both tables (differences of NRE/NRO and PIS/Non PIS) again. I know the technicalities can be a bit overwhelming sometimes.

Now that we know the basic differences between an NRO and an NRE account, it's safe to say an NRE account is more favourable to choose. Solely due to its ease of usage for smooth operations, which we will discuss in the next chapter.

# Chapter 3

# First Step: Open Up an NRE Account

Till now, we've discussed about the major differences between NRO and NRE. And based on the differences we found out that NRE is a better option to begin your investing journey.

And now comes the part where I'd tell you to put all your focus into this chapter as in this chapter we will explain to you the complete structure of how to open an NRE Account to begin your investment journey. The list of complete documentation that's necessary to register yourself as an NRE account holder.

But before that, let's discuss why to choose an NRE account over an NRO.

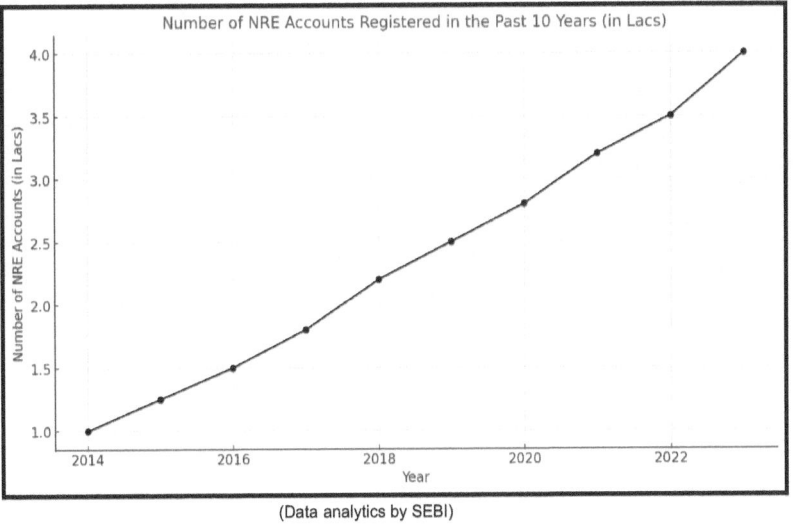

(Data analytics by SEBI)

## 5 Key Benefits of Choosing an NRE Bank Account as an NRI

## 1. Tax Free Income on Investments

One of the most significant advantages of having an NRE account over an NRO is that the interest received on deposits is completely tax-free in India. This includes interest generated on savings and term deposit accounts connected to the NRE account.

This benefit is crucial for NRIs who want to avoid double taxes, particularly in India, because it allows you to boost your earnings without having to worry about Indian tax deductions.

## 2. Repatriation of Funds

As discussed at the end of the previous chapter. That one of the biggest advantages of opting for an NRE account over an NRO is that the capital and interest are entirely repatriable. This means that NRIs can freely move funds, including any interest generated, to their resident nation with no restrictions.

This full repatriation provides flexibility, allowing NRIs to freely transfer funds across borders, which is critical for financial management in many nations.

## 3. Currency Conversion

NRE accounts allow NRIs to maintain their earnings in foreign currencies and convert them into Indian rupees (INR) as necessary, which isn't possible with the NRO accounts.

These accounts make it simple to manage money in multiple currencies, making it ideal for handling costs or investments in India. Simply because the account contains foreign currency deposits, any appreciation in the foreign currency can benefit the account holder.

## 4. Joint accounts with NRIs

An NRE account can be owned jointly, but only with another NRI. This function is especially useful for NRIs who want to manage their finances alongside a spouse, sibling, or business partner who is also an NRI. It enables simple management of joint assets, investments, and family costs.

## 5. Ease of investment in India

An NRE account allows you to invest in mutual funds, equities, and other financial products in India. Funds from the NRE account are approved for investment in the Portfolio Investment Scheme (PIS), allowing NRIs to diversify their investment portfolio in Indian markets.

The tax-free interest and full repatriation make it ideal for NRIs who want to increase their money without the hassle of managing taxable accounts.

These are probably the reasons why the majority of my NRI friends opted for NRE bank accounts to begin their mutual funds investment journey in India. And probably why you as an NRI should too.

That was all with respect to why you need an NRE account. Let's move on to How to set up an NRE Bank Account in India in a few easy steps.

## 1. Required Documents for the Process

- **Passport**: A valid copy of your passport, including the pages with your personal details, photograph, signature, and visa/residence permit.
- **Proof of NRI Status**: This could be a copy of your valid visa, work permit, resident permit, or any other relevant document proving your NRI status.
- **Address Proof**: Proof of your current overseas address, such as a utility bill, rental agreement, or bank statement.
- **Recent Passport-Sized Photographs**: The number can vary depending on the selected bank. Usually, it's 2-4 in total nos.
- **Initial Deposit**: Some banks may require a minimum initial deposit to open your account.

An important note to follow here: All copies of the documents may need to be self-attested and in some cases, notarised.

## 2. Choosing a Bank

After you've gathered the required documents it's now time to choose the bank that you want to set up your NRE account with. The most notable banks that provide an NRE account service in India as of 2024 are:

- ICICI Bank
- HDFC Bank
- IndusInd Bank
- Yes Bank
- PNB Bank
- Kotak Mahindra Bank
- Union Bank of India
- IDFC First
- Indian Bank
- Axis Bank
- SBI Bank

Quality of service may vary from bank to bank. Some people choose the traditional old Govt. Banks like SBI due to their safety features. At the same time, the younger generation tends to lean over Pvt. banks due to their effective customer care service and fewer online server issues compared to a government bank and a better online banking experience overall.

**Note:** Not all banks provide PIS Trading account service. As discussed in the last chapter only a handful of banks facilitate this service and these are:

- HDFC Bank
- ICICI Bank
- Axis Bank
- Yes Bank
- IDFC First Bank
- IndusInd Bank

So to register for a PIS enabled NRE account, you can only choose from the above banks as of 2024.

## 3. Fill out the Bank's Application Form

Download the NRE account application form from your chosen bank's website or request it from a local branch. The form will ask for your personal details, NRI status, and other required information. Make sure to read it carefully to fill it out accurately.

## 4. Submit the Application

You can submit your completed application form and documents via one of the following methods:

- **In-person at a Branch**: If you're in India, you can visit a local branch and submit the documents.
- **Overseas Branch/Office**: Some Indian banks have overseas branches where you can submit the forms.
- **Courier Service**: If you're applying from abroad, you can mail the documents to the bank's NRI division or any specific address provided by the bank.

## 5. Verification of Documents

Once the bank receives your documents, the next step is for the bank to verify these and help you set up your account. The verification process typically lasts up to 5-7 working days. Also depends on bank to bank and the mode you used to submit these documents.

## 6. Account Activation

Once your documents are verified by the bank. It's now time to activate your NRE account. Once your account is approved, you will receive a confirmation from the bank along with your account number and details. You'll also receive login credentials for your online banking activation and other services. Once the account is activated you'll be asked to deposit an initial amount to fully activate the account.

You have to make the deposit in foreign currency and the bank will convert this deposit to INR. You can transfer funds through wire transfer or deposit foreign currency in person if you're in India.

## 7. Start Using the Account

As the account has been set up, you can now transfer funds, make investments, or use the NRE account for any other banking needs. The account is fully repatriable, so you can move funds to and from your resident country with ease.

**Additional Tips:**

- Make sure you maintain compliance with FEMA regulations. FEMA here stands for Foreign Exchange Management Act.

- Use the bank's mobile app or online platform to monitor your account and manage investments.

Here are your complete steps to follow and I can guarantee you that as long as you don't skip a part from the above. The entire process can go smoothly, without a hiccup. So as soon as your NRE bank account is set up, it's now time to set up your PIS in accordance with your NRE Account.

As discussed in the previous chapter, a PIS trading account is needed for the NRIs with an NRE Bank account to facilitate Mutual fund investment. Now we'll discuss the procedure to make your NRE account PIS enabled.

The first step is to open an NRE account which we have already covered above. Now the next step includes:

## 1. Choosing a Bank

As discussed earlier, only a handful of Indian banks actually facilitate such a service, so you need to choose from the ones below:

- HDFC Bank
- ICICI Bank
- Axis Bank
- Yes Bank
- IDFC First Bank
- IndusInd Bank

## 2. Apply for the PIS Permission

You need permission from the Reserve Bank of India (RBI) to open a PIS account. This permission is generally obtained by the bank on your behalf when you apply for a PIS account.

Documents required to open a PIS account:

- **Duly filled PIS application form** (available at your bank)
- **Proof of NRI status** (copy of valid passport, visa, or OCI/PIO card)
- **Proof of overseas address** (e.g., utility bill or foreign bank statement)
- **PAN (Permanent Account Number)** card

- **Passport-size photographs**
- **Cancelled cheque** from your NRE or NRO account (to link with the PIS account)
- **Copy of your FEMA declaration** and **Client Master List (CML)** from your brokerage firm
- **Bank Statement** for the last 6 months or a **net worth certificate**.

## 3. Open a Trading/Demat Account with a Broker

You need to open your trading account with a reliable Stock Broker in India to start investing. Some of the reputable brokers include Zerodha, HDFC Securities, ICICI Direct. The broker and the bank will work together to set up a PIS account linked to your demat account.

This type of PIS-linked demat account can only be opened offline. This means a client has to submit the physical documents to the stock broker to verify his/her credentials. It isn't that difficult as it might sound. One just needs to collect the documents, crosscheck the details carefully for once and mail the physical documents to the broker, and the rest of the communication can be done online.

**Important Note:** NRIs must make sure that their residential status is marked as Non - resident on the ITD website before applying for an account opening with the stock broker.

## 4. Completing Bank Formalities

Once you have submitted the required documents for verification and sign the agreement with the bank. Your bank will send it to the RBI ( Reserve bank of India) for the approval and once they receive the approval. Your PIS Account will be opened.

## 5. Receiving Your PIS Account Details

Upon approval, the bank will provide you with the PIS Account number, which will be used to route your investments and for accessing your bank statement.

**Important Note**: The bank will charge a small fee for filing reports to the RBI. The bank will monitor your transactions and ensure compliance with the Foreign Exchange Management Act (FEMA) and other RBI guidelines. They will also deduct applicable Tax Deducted at Source (TDS) on your gains.

Now that wasn't so hard to grasp as you might have thought about considering complex Indian rules and regulations, was it?

**A Tip:** You may still have some questions about the procedure and your bank can answer these for you. But often when on call or in person we can't seem to remember everything point to point as we try to recall these. So write every query of yours on a piece of paper or as notes on your phone, so you have it at all times with you.

While mutual fund investment in India is relatively straightforward, NRIs have to adhere to specific guidelines. One of which is if an NRI belongs to a FATF Grey list country. They cannot invest in Mutual funds in India.

FATF here stands for Financial Action Task Force and you don't need to go deep into it as to what's the criteria for the countries to end on the list. Just know that there are certain countries that are banned from investing in Mutual funds in India and below is the list of these:

- Bulgaria.
- Burkina Faso.
- Cameroon.
- Croatia.
- Democratic Republic of Congo.
- Haiti.
- Kenya.
- Mali.

So unless you are an NRI from these countries on FATF's grey list, you have nothing to worry about and can safely invest in the Indian Mutual funds market.

Now you have understood the entire procedure in detail to open a PIS enabled NRE account to begin your mutual funds journey in India and build that generational wealth you've always dreamed of. No, really that's it, not only can you now make your future generation remember you with a feeling of being proud about your financial accomplishments that'll be of great benefit for them, but also your partner bank, who wouldn't have to break a sweat in explaining you all these in detail as they normally do and would probably consider you a God send boon, no kidding.

After you've opened the account, now comes the part where you need to know what type of mutual fund to invest in and what are the Mutual funds out there that are to be trusted enough to be invested in for the long term. We'll get to know all about it in our next chapter.

Before we begin our 4th phase of this book, let's recall everything we've learned so far

1. In Chapter 1 we've learned the importance of investing in a dynamic economy such as India, with the highest GDP growth rate amongst all the major economies and an untapped potential that rivals the 90s Chinese economy. We understood why it is the best place to invest not only due to its fast growing economy but also because it is a politically stable democracy, a sign of safe investment.

2. In Chapter 2, we learnt the basics of opening a demat account for NRIs to invest in Mutual funds in India. The kind of accounts NRI needs to start investing. We discussed the difference between NRO & NRE accounts as well as PIS and Non PIS accounts. And also how an NRE account would be beneficial for most NRIs due to no policy on your investment and full credit repatriation facility available with this account.

3. In Chapter 3, we learned about how to open an NRE Bank account and which banks to choose with respect to a PIS NRE account. Also, the complete documentation required for your NRE bank account and the PIS enabled demat account with your stock broker. And at last, the countries under FATF's grey list from where the people are barred from investing in the Indian market.

# Chapter 4

# Why Mutual Funds and Regular SIPs in Mutual Funds

Well, so far we've discussed how to begin investing in Mutual funds. Why to invest in India and its market. But in Indian markets, there are more options involved like stocks, commodities etc. Why do we keep our focus on Mutual funds and not on company stocks that can yield an even higher return? Although we have discussed the benefits of mutual funds in the previous chapter, it still begs the question of, why is it only a guide for Mutual Funds and why doesn't it cover other high returns options like Stocks. Let's get to know this in brief.

## Why Should NRIs Choose Mutual Funds Investment over Stocks

To each his own, both have their own merits but when it comes to choosing a better one from the two, Mutual Funds have a clear edge for an NRI investment plan, here's why:

### 1. Managed by the Experts

In a typical Mutual Funds investment, your money is pooled with other investors and the investment is handled by experienced fund managers. These years of experience give them an edge over an average investor like yourselves who might try to invest in the stock market after watching some YouTube videos, some online insights or reading through the chart patterns etc. but in case you have invested in any kind of stocks you know it's not that easy as it looks. None of these things can help you generate good returns over a long period of time and you're more prone to losing money than making it.

Investing in the market is one thing but being able to get constant great returns from it, is another. So that's where your experienced fund managers step in. Experience matters when it comes to investing and going with someone whose only job has been generating good returns for their clients over the years, is usually a better approach than a DIY scenario in this case.

### 2. Diversified Portfolio

Investing in Mutual Funds gives you access to a diversified portfolio. But why choose a diversified portfolio in the first place? Well, keeping all your eggs in one basket risks being broken all at once in case of an accident. Similarly, not diversifying your portfolio and keeping all your investment in one place can make you lose more than you expect in case of a market panic.

Mutual Funds are made up of a diversified portfolio that contains stocks, bonds, government securities etc. This reduces the risk of your investment losing its value in case one industry sector goes down in the stock market. For those who can't spend hours researching the market every single day, this type of diversified investment is a better, safer choice.

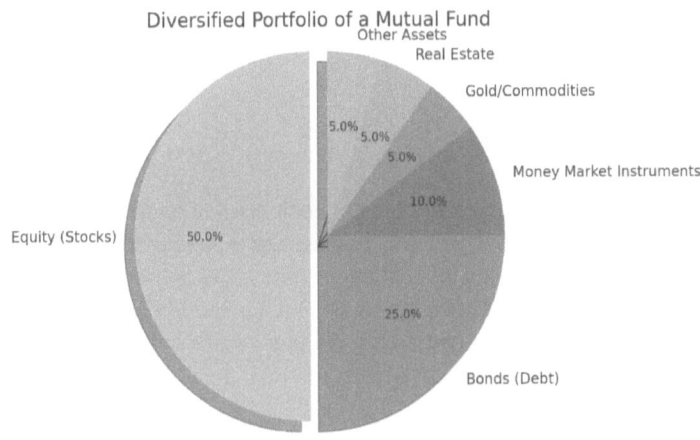

## 3. Lower Commitment Value

As discussed above, in order to generate constant returns in the financial market one needs experience with the market trends, the right knowledge to book your profits and the biggest of all, time. Time is of extreme essence here. So when you invest in Mutual Funds, you don't have to monitor it constantly like your stock investment.

When you invest with one of the best fund managers who have a track record of providing great returns, you can rest assured your investment is safe and sound and you won't need to spend your valuable time monitoring it.

Telling you this from my personal experience, the more you look at your investment, the more anxious you get about it and this can only help you gain anxiety rather than some peace.

## 4. Option for SIPs (Systematic Investment Plan)

This is the best part about investing in Mutual Funds. SIPs mean that you don't have to put together all your initial investment in one go. You can invest bit by bit in regular intervals, it can be weekly or monthly. And reach your goal of financial gains systematically.

In contrast to stock market investment where you often need a lump sum amount to begin your investment journey, here with a Mutual Funds SIP you can simply put together a fixed amount weekly or monthly (totally depends on you) and watch your investment go, safely and steadily.

## 5. A Cost Effective Investment

When you trade in stocks you may be charged a convenience fee each time you sell and buy stocks. But with Mutual Funds you only pay a small management fee once which in long term beats stocks in terms of cost effectiveness. And there's one more benefit attached to making a payment once and making it a dozen times over and over. It's easier to track that one payment than the payment that's getting deducted multiple times.

Often, it's these multiple small charges that lead to a much bigger loss on a person's overall investment.

So, think smart, think Mutual Funds. Now that's the motto I personally have been following for a long time. Ever since I've learned the benefit of a long term investment and got out of my dream world of finding that one stock that could turn my investment a thousand folds in a short period of time.

Now that we are certain of choosing Mutual Funds for our investment plan. Let's get to know the type of Mutual Funds in which one can choose to invest in and also the Mutual Funds on the market that may be suited best for you.

# Types of Mutual Funds in India

Generally, there are 2 types of Mutual Funds most people invest in. These are Equity and Debt Mutual Funds. You mostly need to know only about these two, but just to give you complete info on this subject, I'll feature all of the types that exist for investment. So you can decide what suits you the best.

I'll also mention the R&R (returns and risk) factor associated with these.

## 1. Equity Mutual Funds

These are the mutual funds that provide one with the highest returns in the Mutual Funds market. Here fund managers typically invest in high returns yielding assets. These are great for both short-term and long-term growth. And since these provide high returns, the risk associated with these types of Mutual Funds tends to be higher than the rest.

Although compared to other kinds of investments such as Stocks, Real Estate etc. it's very low.

These can be further classified as:

- **Large Cap Funds:** These types of funds invest in well-established, large companies with stable returns.

- **Mid Cap & Small Cap Funds:** Medium-sized or smaller companies are the target here, and these may offer higher growth potential but carry more risk.

- **Sectoral Thematic Funds:** Industries like Technology, Banking or Healthcare are specific preferences of these kinds of funds.

- **ELSS (Equity Linked Savings Scheme):** People primarily invest in these for the tax benefit it offers. This fund offers you tax benefits under section 80C for a lock-in period of 3 years (Not beneficial to an NRI with NRE bank account)

## 2. Debt Mutual Funds

This is a type of Mutual funds that's suited for long-term growth as it provides you with stable, low to no-risk options. But with a low-risk option comes low returns. This type of Mutual Funds has a portfolio of government, corporate bonds and corporate debt securities. A low return but the safest investment option.

These can be further categorised as:

- **Liquid Funds:** Invest in short-term instruments with a maturity period of up to 91 days, providing liquidity and lower risk.

- **Income Funds:** Focus on bonds with longer maturity periods, offering higher returns with moderate risk.

- **Gilt Funds:** Invest primarily in government securities, ensuring minimal credit risk.

Now these are the primary types of mutual funds you may choose from, depending on your returns appetite and the risk tolerance. We'll also discuss some other types of Mutual Funds that have developed a new interest in the eyes of investors.

## 3. Hybrid Mutual Funds

As the name suggests, this type of Mutual Funds is a mix of Equity and Debt. This means the portfolio in these types of funds includes a mix of the industries that equity and debt mutual funds are made up of. So these type of funds provides you with a balance between the two worlds. Sound returns with a stable risk factor.

The 3 Types of Hybrid Funds are:

- **Balanced Funds:** These Funds have investments in both stocks and bonds. Usually in the equity to debt ratio of 60:40.

- **Aggressive Hybrid Funds:** It has more emphasis on equity. With up to 75-80% of investment in stocks.

- **Conservative Hybrid Funds:** These have a higher preference for debt instruments and invest a smaller portion in equities. Such a tool of investment is suited for investors with the lowest risk tendencies.

## 4. Index Funds

Index funds replicate and track a particular stock market index, such as Nifty 50 or Sensex. It looks to track the performance of the index. Since it is a passively managed fund, it reflects the index it tracks. As there isn't much management involved, the fees are relatively low, so it is an inexpensive affair.

## 5. Global Funds

International or global funds invest in foreign markets, to offer a kind of diversification beyond domestic investments. These funds allow Indian investors to participate in the growth of global markets and hedge against domestic market risks.

## 6. FOFs (Funds of Funds)

FoFs invest in other mutual funds rather than directly in stocks or bonds. This allows for diversification across different fund types, managers, and strategies. Think of it as a hybrid on hybrid. (Now don't you giggle making out the other meaning of it)

These are the types of your typical Mutual Funds in India. It's up to your investment and returns requirements which one you choose to invest in. While each of these varies in risk and returns. Though all of these are a safer investment bet than other high-yield investment options.

After discussing the types of Mutual Funds to invest in, now comes the part where we talk about famous Asset Management Companies or Mutual Funds Companies in India. We'll talk about the best performing fund companies in the 2 primary Mutual Fund types, which are Equity and Debt Mutual Funds. Yay Boi, here comes the money.

## Top 3 Best Performing Equity Mutual Funds

Below are the best performing Equity Mutual Funds based on their per annum returns for the past 5 years, including a total analysis of their fund structure.

**Source** - Groww ( A leading stock broker for Mutual fund investing in India) I'm not promoting Groww here, it's just that I use it for my own mutual fund investing. Data from 2024.

## 1. Quant Small Cap Fund Direct Plan Growth

- **Fund Size** - 25534 Cr. INR
- **Annual Returns** - 50.47% Per annum  (For the Past 5 Years)
- **Min. SIP Amount** - 1000 INR
- **Risk Factor** - Medium to High Risk
- **Current Holdings** - 80

**Holding Analysis:**

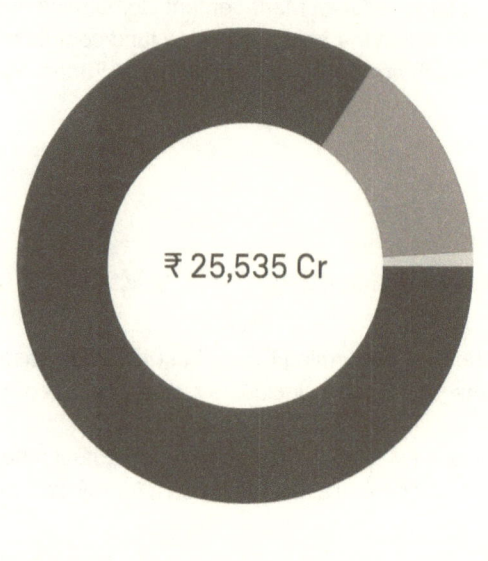

Equity / Debt / Cash split

₹ 25,535 Cr

- Equity **84.2%**
- Cash **14.7%**
- Debt **0.9%**

Equity sector allocation

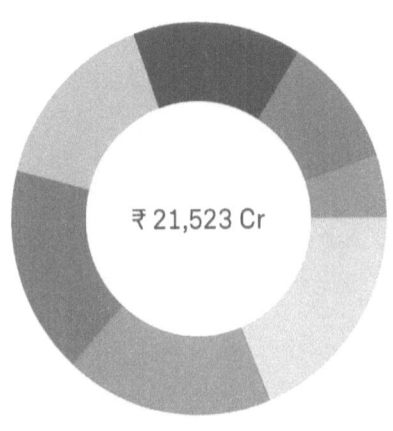

₹ 21,523 Cr

| | | | | |
|---|---|---|---|---|
| ● Others | 18.8% | ● Services | 18% |
| ● Healthcare | 17.2% | ● Energy | 15.4% |
| ● Financial | 14.5% | ● Consume... | 10.8% |
| ● Communic... | 5.1% | | |

☐ **Overview:** It's a mid to high risk best performing fund when viewed as a long term investment. So if you're a long term investor and have the tendency to accept risk, then this is one of the best funds for you to invest in for long term high growth. And yes it's also my personal favourite. I know a bit of risk involved in such high returns funds, but so far it hasn't disappointed.

## 2. Motilal Oswal Midcap Fund Direct Growth

- **Fund Size** - 15,940 Cr. INR
- **Annual Returns** - 38.73% Per Annum (For the Past 5 Years)
- **Min. SIP Amount** - 500 INR
- **Risk Factor** - Medium Risk
- **Current Holdings** - 20

**Holding Analysis:**

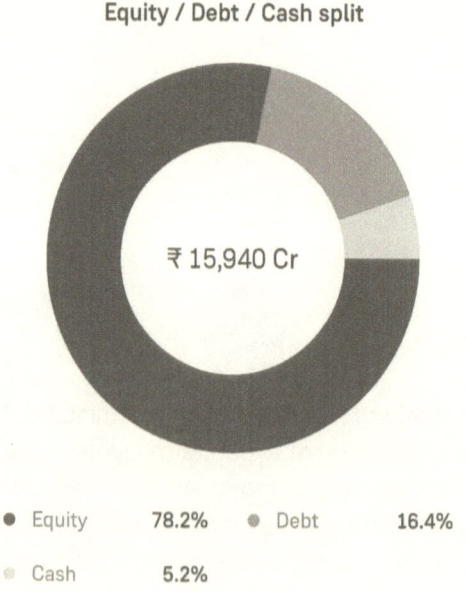

Equity / Debt / Cash split

₹ 15,940 Cr

- Equity  78.2%
- Debt  16.4%
- Cash  5.2%

## Equity sector allocation

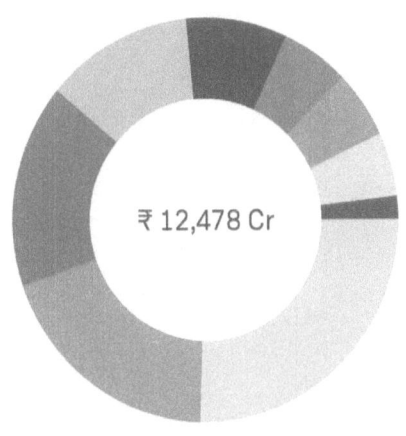

₹ 12,478 Cr

| | | | | |
|---|---|---|---|---|
| ● Technolo... | 25.5% | | ● Consume... | 19.3% |
| ● Capital G... | 16.3% | | ● Automob... | 12.3% |
| ● Financial | 8.4% | | ● Healthcare | 5.6% |
| ● Chemicals | 5.4% | | ● Services | 5.1% |
| ● Others | 1.8% | | | |

*Holdings as of: 31 Aug 2024

☐ **Overview:** It's a mid risk 2nd best performing fund in my list. You will find some Mutual Funds that deliver twice the returns as this one here, but that's only for a short period (3 - 12 months) So if you're a long term investor and have the tendency to accept some risk. This is one of the best funds for you to invest in for long term high growth.

## 3. ICICI Prudential Infrastructure Fund

- **Fund Size** - 6142 Cr. INR
- **Annual Returns** - 36.8% Per Annum (For the Past 5 Years)
- **Min. SIP Amount** - 100 INR
- **Risk Factor** - Medium Risk
- **Current Holdings** - 62

**Holding Analysis:**

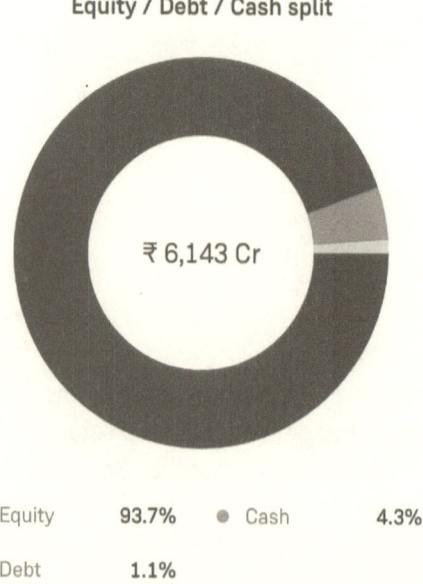

Equity / Debt / Cash split

₹ 6,143 Cr

- Equity — 93.7%
- Cash — 4.3%
- Debt — 1.1%

Equity sector allocation

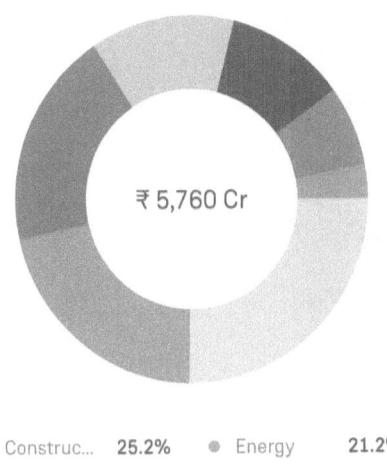

₹ 5,760 Cr

| | | | | |
|---|---|---|---|---|
| ○ Construc... | 25.2% | ● Energy | 21.2% |
| ● Financial | 19.2% | ● Metals &... | 13.2% |
| ● Capital G... | 10.9% | ● Services | 7% |
| ● Others | 2.9% | | |

☐ **Overview:** It's a mid risk high performing fund. ICICI is amongst one of the major banks in India so it has a reputation to maintain, hence, its small fund cap that comes with mid risk can be trusted for long term. Especially due to its pretty good returns of 36% per annum for 5 years.

# Top 3 Best Performing Debt Mutual Funds

Below are some of the low risk best performing debt mutual funds. Their ranking has been calculated on their risk factor and their per annum returns for the past 5 years.

## 1. SBI Magnum Gilt Fund

- **Fund Size** - 6142 Cr. INR
- **Annual Returns** - 7.8% Per Annum (For the Past 5 Years)
- **Min. SIP Amount** - 500 INR
- **Risk Factor** - Low Risk
- **Current Holdings** - 5

**Holding Analysis:**

**Equity/Debt/Cash Split**

Debt - 96.2%

Cash - 3.7%

**Debt Sector Allocation**

Sovereign - 96.2%

Others - 3.7%

**Overview:** For those who have no tolerance for risk in their investments. Here comes low risk, Mid. Returns Debt Mutual Fund. This is one of the most trusted Debt funds amongst major investors and provides a decent 7.8% annual return.

## 2. HDFC Regular Savings Fund Direct Growth

- **Fund Size** - 5433 Cr. INR

- **Annual Returns** - 8.94% Per Annum (For the Past 5 Years)

- **Min. SIP Amount** - 300 INR

- **Risk Factor** - Low Risk

- **Current Holdings** - 117

Holding Analysis:

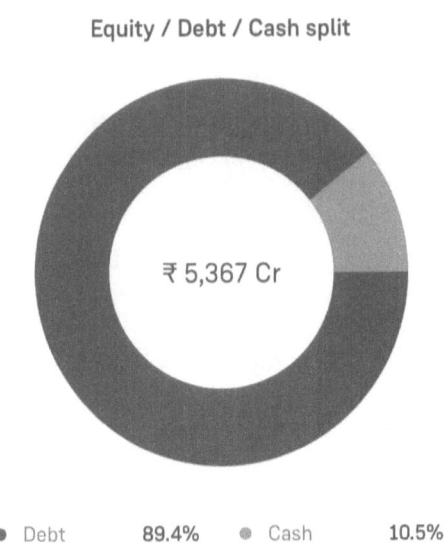

HDFC Regular Savings Fund Direct Growth

Equity / Debt / Cash split

₹ 5,367 Cr

● Debt     89.4%    ● Cash     10.5%

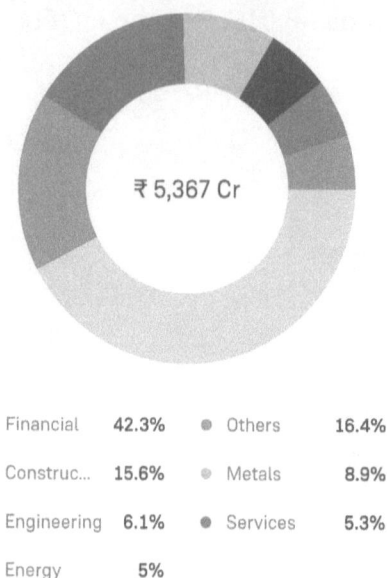

Debt sector allocation

₹ 5,367 Cr

- Financial — 42.3%
- Construc... — 15.6%
- Engineering — 6.1%
- Energy — 5%
- Others — 16.4%
- Metals — 8.9%
- Services — 5.3%

**Overview:** A Debt mutual fund with a huge variety of holdings and slightly better return than the first. A wise choice to invest in, especially for a diversified portfolio even in a debt fund.

## 3. Aditya Birla Sun Life Dynamic Bond Retail Fund Direct Growth

- **Fund Size** - 1687 Cr. INR
- **Annual Returns** - 6.38% Per Annum (For the Past 5 Years)
- **Min. SIP Amount** - 1000 INR
- **Risk Factor** - Low Risk
- **Current Holdings** - 26

**Holding Analysis:**

**Equity/Debt/Cash Split**

Debt - 98.8%

Cash - 1.1%

**Debt Sector Allocation**

Sovereign - 91.8%

Others - 8.1%

**Overview:** A trusted debt fund with nominal returns of just over 6 %. Their holding structure is like most debt funds, less diversified. But is a low risk fund and highly trusted. Which makes it one of the top 3 debt funds to have.

So these are your top performing Mutual Funds for 2024, rankings were based on their trustworthy factor and their past 5 years returns. Now you know the difference between different types of Mutual Funds and at the same time the list of best performing Mutual Funds both in Equity and Debt. Personally, I prefer equity over debt funds because, what's there in a bit of risk, since we put our lives into more risks just by doing usual chores every single day but to each his own. Both kinds of investments serve different purposes for different people.

I'm not the one to force down my opinion, all I can do is provide you the right knowledge for these. So when the time comes you can make the right financial decision, not just for yourself but for your future generation.

**Note:** If this was a YouTube video I would be forced to post this disclaimer, although it isn't one but still let me put it right here: Mutual Funds Market is subject to risk, please read the investment related documents carefully before investing.

If this small line puts a doubt in your mind, just remember, we put our lives more at risk by doing something as safe as taking a shower every day. :)

Risks are everywhere, we just need to be willing to accept the ones we understand completely.

---------------------------------∞--------------------------------------------

# Chapter 5

# Navigating the Rules: SEBI and Investor Protection for NRI

Just like the U.S. has the SEC as the enforcement agency for its financial market, India has SEBI (Securities and Exchange Board for India) as its market regulator. SEBI plays a crucial role in protecting investor's money by enacting laws to maintain the integrity of the market and ensure compliance.

Making sure everyone follows the rules and regulations and those failing to do so, have to face the wrath of the SEBI department and are punished accordingly as per law.

In this chapter, we'll understand the SEBIs regulation framework for the NRIs and as an NRI how you can trust SEBI to keep your investment safe. But before that let's get an overview of SEBIs history in India.

## History of SEBI

SEBI was first introduced in 1988 as a non statutory body for regulating the securities market in India. It was in 1992 that SEBI became a statutory body and gained autonomous power as the Govt. passed the SEBI Act.

SEBI has its headquarters in Mumbai and also has regional offices in New Delhi, Kolkata, Chennai and Ahmedabad. It is governed by a board that's comprised of the following individuals:

- A chairman appointed by the Union Government of India.
- Two representatives from the Union Finance Ministry.
- One representative from the Reserve Bank of India.
- Five additional members, nominated by the Union Government, of which at least three must serve as full-time members.

Following a 1999 amendment, SEBI was granted oversight of collective investment schemes, with the exception of nidhis, chit funds, and cooperative societies.

Its Key functions include:

1. SEBI regulates all financial operations in India, including mutual funds.

2. It ensures fair practices, prevents fraud, and responds to malpractices to safeguard investors.

3. Acts as a watchdog to make sure that stock exchanges, brokers, and other intermediaries operate smoothly.

4. Develops criteria for investments such as mutual funds to ensure a secure investment environment.

These were the basics you needed to know about SEBI, the watchdog for the financial market in India. Now let's talk about its regulations in place that can assure you as an NRI to invest your hard earned money in the Indian market.

## How SEBI Protects Your Mutual Fund Investment

SEBI's regulations are designed to provide a secure investment experience for both domestic as well as international investors including our very own NRI group. Let's take a look at some of its policies through which it ensures protection for the NRI investors in the mutual fund market

1. Keeping Transparency and Disclosure Requirements

It is mandatory for SEBI to provide full disclosure of all information related to mutual fund schemes. This includes the investment strategy, risk factors, past performance, and associated costs (such as expense ratios). NRIs can access this information through mutual fund offer documents, ensuring that they make informed decisions.

☐ **Why It's Important for NRIs**: Since NRIs invest from abroad, it makes it more important to have clear visibility into their investments. SEBI is here to make sure that the NRIs are not kept in the dark about how their money is being managed.

2. Fair Dealing with Investors

SEBI ensures that all mutual funds in India operate on the principles of fairness and equality. Every investor, including NRIs, has equal rights and access to investment opportunities, and all dealings are conducted in a non-discriminatory manner.

> ☐ **Why It's Important for NRIs**: NRIs often worry about being at a disadvantage compared to domestic investors. SEBI assures them that this is not the case, allowing NRIs to invest in the Indian market with confidence.

## 3. Prevention of Malpractices

SEBI actively works to curb fraudulent schemes, insider trading, and market manipulation. It has stringent mechanisms to investigate suspicious activities and enforce penalties against those who break the rules.

> ☐ **Why It's Important for NRIs**: Given the distance and the fact that NRIs may not be directly involved in the Indian market, the fear of fraud can be higher. SEBI's role in preventing malpractices reassures NRIs that their investments are safe.

## 4. Risk Management

SEBI enforces strict risk management guidelines for mutual funds. Fund managers must maintain a certain level of liquidity to meet redemption requests, and diversification is encouraged to reduce risk.

> ☐ **Why It's Important for NRIs**: NRIs may not have regular access to their portfolios, so they rely on fund managers to handle risks. SEBI's rules ensure that these manager's investment decisions are taken carefully which can help safeguard investor's interests.

## 5. Grievance Redressal Mechanism

SEBI has put in place a robust grievance redressal system for investors. If NRIs face any issues with their mutual fund investments, such as mismanagement or fraud, they can file complaints with SEBI. The complaints are handled through SEBI's centralised grievance portal, SCORES (SEBI Complaints Redress System).

> ☐ **Why It's Important for NRIs**: NRIs often feel disconnected from the Indian market. A strong grievance redressal system ensures that their concerns are heard and acted upon, even from abroad.

As we've discussed the assurances that SEBI provides to keep your confidence high when it comes to investing in the country. Let's get to know more about the topic, for eg. the regulations it has for NRIs investing in Mutual Funds. Nothing to worry about, just some small things to keep in check that we've already discussed in the previous chapters as well in brief.

Let's read the short outlines on the same. This will also jog your memory about the previously read stuff in this book and help you decide if you've been reading everything carefully here or if most of the things are just going over your head.

## SEBI's Regulations for NRIs Investing in Mutual Funds

SEBI has specific guidelines that NRIs must follow when investing in Indian mutual funds. These guidelines are designed to ensure that the investment process is streamlined, transparent, and secure for NRIs.

### 1. KYC Compliance for NRIs

Before NRIs can invest in mutual funds, they must complete the Know Your Customer (KYC) process. SEBI has made KYC mandatory to verify the identity of investors and prevent money laundering.

- **Steps for KYC**:
    1. NRIs must submit copies of their passport, visa, and overseas address proof.
    2. They must also provide bank account details (NRE or NRO) that will be linked to the mutual fund account.
    3. The KYC process can be completed online, through authorised agents, or at Indian consulates abroad.

- **Why They Make You Do This?**: KYC ensures the legitimacy of investments and prevents illegal activities. For NRIs, it provides a layer of protection against identity theft and other fraudulent practices.

### 2. Repatriation of Funds

SEBI has clear rules regarding the repatriation of funds invested in mutual funds by NRIs. As discussed in the previous chapters, funds invested through an NRE (Non-Resident External) account can be repatriated, meaning the entire principal and earnings can be sent back to the NRI's country of residence.

However, as we already know (if you've been reading this book carefully) that the investments made through an NRO (Non-Resident Ordinary) account are non-repatriable beyond a certain limit.

- **Why Such a Regulation?**: NRIs need clarity on the rules governing how they can withdraw and transfer funds internationally. SEBI ensures that these rules are easy to follow and transparent, allowing NRIs to plan their financial strategies effectively.

## 3. Taxation and TDS

While SEBI doesn't directly govern tax regulations, it plays a role in ensuring compliance with tax laws. Tax Deducted at Source (TDS) is applicable to NRI mutual fund investments, particularly on dividends and capital gains. SEBI ensures that mutual fund houses follow these tax laws and deduct the necessary amounts.

- **Why It's Important?**: NRIs must be aware of the tax implications of their investments to avoid penalties or legal issues. SEBI's role in enforcing these regulations helps NRIs stay compliant with Indian tax laws.

Now tell me honestly, did you feel like you already knew all these or did you feel like you're reading this for the first time? No worries, I trust you. You've been a good reader and I'm assured that I have all your attention in place. You see, understanding every detail provided in the book is of the essence as most people lose money or trap themselves in financial frauds only due to the ignorance of rules and frameworks to help you as an investor.

## SEBI's Efforts for Investor's Education

To further reduce the chances of risks involved with your particular investments, SEBI has launched a few initiatives to help with increased market awareness among investors to help build a strong investor base in India. This effort becomes even more important for the NRIs.

Let's take a look at some of these initiatives:

### Investor Awareness Programs

SEBI conducts a wide range of Investor Awareness Programs designed to reach a broad spectrum of investors, including NRIs. These programs include workshops, seminars, and campaigns aimed at simplifying complex financial products and ensuring that investors understand the basics of mutual funds, stock markets, and other investment avenues.

These events are often organised in collaboration with financial institutions, mutual fund houses, and intermediaries, and are conducted both in India and abroad. For NRIs, especially those residing in countries with large Indian communities like the UAE, the UK, and the USA, these initiatives can be invaluable in bridging the knowledge gap.

The workshops focus on understanding financial products, risks, returns, and the process of investing in India. They also offer guidance on taxation rules and regulatory frameworks that apply to NRI investments.

## Online Resourceful Platforms

With the growing use of digital platforms, SEBI has expanded its online resources to cater to tech-savvy investors. On SEBI's official website, you can access a treasure trove of information ranging from basic investment principles to detailed regulatory guidelines on mutual funds, stock markets, and other financial products.

This website (www.sebi.gov.in) includes:

☐ Detailed information on different mutual fund schemes, their performance, and how NRIs can participate in them.

☐ Step-by-step guides on opening Demat accounts, choosing between NRE and NRO accounts, and navigating the complexities of Portfolio Investment Schemes (PIS).

☐ Educational materials such as brochures, articles, and reports on best practices in investing, risk management, and compliance with Indian regulations.

By providing NRIs with the right guidance, SEBI ensures they have easy access to trustworthy sources for understanding India's financial landscape.

## Interactive Tools for Quick Answers

In addition to static information, SEBI offers various interactive tools on its website to enhance the decision-making process for investors. These tools are designed to simplify complex calculations and provide instant answers to common investment-related queries. Some key tools include:

- **Investment Calculators**: SEBI provides calculators that help NRIs estimate potential returns on their mutual fund investments, calculate Systematic Investment Plan (SIP) returns, and even project retirement savings. These calculators are easy to use and allow investors to make data-driven decisions about their investment strategies.

- **Frequently Asked Questions (FAQs)**: SEBI's website features an extensive FAQ section that covers various aspects of investing in India, including taxation rules, how NRIs can repatriate their funds, and regulatory requirements for mutual fund investments.

The FAQs are particularly helpful in addressing common concerns and queries NRIs may have about investing in India.

- **Portfolio Tracking**: For NRIs managing multiple investments, portfolio tracking tools are available to help them keep an eye on the performance of their investments and assess whether they align with their financial goals.

As we approach the end of this chapter I hope your doubts are cleared with regards to a strict regulation in place to protect your investments. In this chapter we've learned about the importance of SEBI, its roles, its various regulations in place and what these mean for you as an NRI.

We also learned about the initiatives that SEBI has taken to ensure more awareness for an investor.

So every kind of investor, whether domestic or international, would find India a secure place to invest.

# Chapter 6

# How to Invest While Living Abroad: A Look at Some Smart Strategies

The past 5 chapters dealt with the basics of investing in Mutual Funds. Which are your typical starter points to open a trading account, rules and regulations for investing, the types of Mutual Funds etc. And now in this chapter, we'll look at some investing strategies one can adopt to invest in Mutual Funds in India as an NRI. Some expert strategies that you can implement from any part of the world and can make investments in a much safer way.

## Some Smart Investment Strategies for Mutual Funds Investment

### 1. Utilising Online Platforms for Monitoring

Being far from your invested place of interest doesn't mean it has to be difficult to keep up with your investment portfolio. These days one can easily keep a track of their investment, and their entire portfolio by the means of financial websites and apps. And Mutual Fund brokers in India provide their in house app with all the technicals that can help you track your portfolio with ease.

Make sure to monitor your investment systematically. It can be once a week, a month or a quarter year. Such a step can help make sure that your investment growth is completely aligned with your financial goals.

## 2. Subscribe to Financial Newsletters

Although there's no right way to time the market every single time. But staying updated with the market trends and regulations can help big time taking the right decisions for your investment. For eg. - Suppose Govt. has increased duties on the sale of steel, and a large part of your investment is in a fund that has invested largely into this industry, then it would be the right time to move your investment from there for a short while to save the gains you've achieved on your investment.

## 3. Take Advantage of Automation

Automation isn't just there for vehicles, chat box etc. it's there in the financial market as well. Although I wouldn't recommend these highly due to their limited learning and though they could save you from some losses in the short run, there's no guarantee that these will be able to perform efficiently in the future as well.

But still you can use some features with respect to automation in case you're busy enough to do the little things yourself. One of such features includes 'Auto Rebalancing'. With automated rebalancing, your portfolio is adjusted periodically to maintain your desired asset allocation.

This keeps your risk in check and makes sure that you are neither too exposed to high-risk investments nor too conservative to give your investment a steady growth.

## The Power of Compounding

Compounding is what builds up your investment in the long run. As Albert Einstein once said, 'Compound interest is the eighth wonder of the world. He who understands it, earns it; he who doesn't, pays it.'

Now I know what you might be thinking, what does Einstein have to do with the financial market but he was a genius right? But Warren Buffet too has said something similar many times with regards to compounding and its long term effects.

Since he was the one who managed to grow a fortune using the same principle. The longer your money stays invested the more powerful the compounding effect becomes.

Now let's understand how compounding actually works with respect to different time horizons.

## After 5 Years of Investing

In the first five years, compounding may seem slow. If you invest ₹1,00,000 at an average return of 30% per year (delivered by the best performing mutual funds) after five years, your investment will grow to approximately ₹3,71,293. While the growth is visible and these are pretty good results to be honest but the real magic of compounding happens over longer periods. Let's check them out.

## After 10 Years of Investing

After 10 years, the effects of compounding become more apparent. With the same 30% annual returns, your ₹1,00,000 investment will grow to ₹13,78,432 more than tripling in value. The magic that's taking place here is of the returns that start accelerating as the interest earned in earlier years itself starts generating additional returns.

## After 15 Years of Investing

At the 15-year mark, compounding really takes off and shows dramatic results. Your ₹1,00,000 will now grow to ₹51,05,100 at 30% annual returns. This is where you start seeing extraordinary growth in wealth. As your wealth with some luck, is now 50 times of what you invested in, in just 15 years.

That's a significantly higher return than 90% of stocks in the world.

## After 20 years of Investing

Now this is the stage where you'd feel like you have a wealth building machine as by this time period your wealth will have turned into a fortune. And this is a time where most people plan to retire if they have been safely investing for a period of 20 years or more. Now how much would you like your ₹1,00,000 investment to have grown by now?

Well, taking into account the compounding formula with an average 30% return, your investment will now have turned to 1,83,09,303 by now. That's 189 times your invested amount. And a bigger return than 99% of the stocks ever gave in the entire history of the financial market.

Now 30% Per annum is a big return, although some rare Mutual Funds have been delivering such returns since a decade but still, such a big return could favour only the luckiest ones. But suppose it's not 30% but 25% or 20% (the average annual return of half of the Mutual Funds in India) So you'd get probably 70-100 times your investment in 20 years. Wouldn't that still be fantastic returns? Well, in my opinion, they most definitely are.

## Understanding the Rule of 72

The Rule of 72 is a simple formula to estimate how long it will take for your investment to double at a given rate of return. You divide 72 by the annual rate of return, and the result is the number of years it will take for your investment to double.

**Formula:**

$$\text{Time to Double (in years)} = \frac{72}{\text{Rate of Return}}$$

**Example:**

If you expect a return of 25% annually on your mutual fund investment, the time required to double your investment is:

$$\text{Time to Double (in years)} = \frac{72}{25} = 2.88 \text{ Years}$$

This means, with a 25% return, your investment will double in approx. every 2.88 years. The Rule of 72 is indeed a handy tool for every investor, especially for you as an NRI, to quickly assess how your investments are growing over time, so you could set realistic expectations that aligns with your financial goals.

## How SIPs in Mutual Funds Can Help with the Compounding Effect for Your Investment

Systematic Investment Plan (SIP) has emerged as the most effective way to invest in Mutual Funds. In fact, 86% of Indians who have invested in Mutual Funds, did it in the form of SIPs. In 2024, SIP inflows in Mutual funds account for over 24000 crores INR ($4.3 Billion AUD). So looking at the data I think it's safe to say that SIP (Systematic Investment Plan) is the most convenient and effective way to invest in Mutual Funds. Especially for those looking for long term wealth creation but lack the required lump sum amount to invest. Investing with SIP also teaches an investor the disciplined and structured method of investing. But how does an SIP help with the compounding effect? Let's talk about that.

1. By investing in SIPs, you regularly contribute to your Mutual Fund investment systematically. Irrespective of the market's position, whether it's on the rise or fall, you're investing consistently. That helps you leverage the bad timing of the market as you're able to buy the units for a cheaper price during the downtime of the market.

Vice-versa you can do the same with respect to buying fewer units when the price is high. Hence, averaging your purchase in a lot more efficient way than lump sum investing.

2. When it comes to compounding, time is of the utmost essence. The best time to invest was yesterday. So the earlier you start, the more time your investments have to grow exponentially. Contributions don't need to be huge to make an impact on your returns. Even small contributions made regularly over long periods can grow into significant amounts.

For those who can't spend much time monitoring the markets frequently but want to leverage the growth potential of Indian Mutual Funds over time, SIPs are the most effective tool set.

3. The returns you earn from SIPs are reinvested in the same mutual fund, adding to your principal amount. This means your future returns will be earned not only on your initial investments but also on the returns that have been reinvested.

This compounding effect becomes more prominent as time goes on, boosting the growth of your investment.

These were a few points to illustrate the role SIP plays in compounding effect. Another important and maybe the most significant feature of SIPs is its ease of setting it up.

With SIPs, you get the feature of auto deductions. So you no longer have to worry about missing your timely payments.

## Investing via Self-Managed Super Fund (SMSF) for Australian NRIs

An SMSF is a type of superannuation fund where the members are also the trustees, giving them full control over how the fund is managed and invested. In short, it's a fund that you manage yourself. Unlike regular superannuation funds managed by financial institutions, SMSFs provide greater flexibility in choosing the types of assets to invest in, including mutual funds in India.

For NRIs living in Australia, investing through a Self-Managed Super Fund (SMSF) can be a smart strategy to manage wealth for those who would like to take advantage of Australia's favourable tax and retirement savings system.

Let me break it down for you to help you understand why and how you as an NRI can invest in mutual funds via SMSFs:

### Key Benefits of Using SMSFs for Indian Investments

- **Tax Benefits:** SMSFs allow you to save for retirement in a tax-effective environment. While your investments are accumulating, the fund's earnings are taxed at a concessional rate of 15%, and once you reach the retirement phase, there may be no tax on your pension income at all.

- **Flexibility with Investment Choice:** You can choose a broad range of investments, including mutual funds in India, giving you control over where your retirement savings are directed.

- **Total Control & Customisation Option:** You can tailor your investment strategy to meet your long-term goals, including investing in sectors or countries where you have a deep understanding or feel confident about the returns.

So these were the few benefits attached to investing in SMSF, now comes the part where I'll teach you how to set up your Self Managed Super Fund. (I have to say it term seems like a trust fund for superheroes)

To set up an SMSF all you have to do is:

## 1. Create The Fund

The first step in setting up a Self-Managed Super Fund (SMSF) is to establish a trust. This step involves appointing trustees (which could be individual trustees or a corporate trustee) who will manage the fund.

It's essential to register your SMSF with the Australian Tax Office (ATO) to ensure it complies with their rules and regulations. The fund must operate solely for providing retirement benefits for its members, and any investment made must align with this purpose.

All the SMSF activities, including investments, must adhere to the trust deed, which is a legal document outlining the operations of the fund.

## 2. Transfer Your Superannuation Savings

After the SMSF is created, the next step is to transfer your superannuation savings from your existing super account into the SMSF since the SMSF acts as a central place where your super funds will be managed. Once the money is transferred, it becomes part of the SMSF pool, which will be used for investing and growing your retirement savings.

For NRIs, it's critical to understand the transfer limits, taxation implications, and ensure that the transfer process complies with ATO guidelines.

## 3. Investment Strategy

A strong investment strategy is crucial to the success of your SMSF. The strategy that you choose to implement should clearly define your investment goals, risk tolerance, and the types of assets you want to invest in.

As an NRI, you have the flexibility to diversify your portfolio internationally. This includes the Indian mutual funds which can provide exposure to a growing market, potentially leading to higher returns.

However, one has to make sure that the investments meet the criteria set out by the ATO, ensuring they serve the best interest of your retirement. This adopted strategy should be reviewed regularly to adapt to market changes and personal circumstances.

## 4. Compliance

Once your SMSF is operational, you must ensure ongoing compliance with the ATO regulations. This includes adhering to contribution caps, managing withdrawals correctly (as they are strictly regulated), and ensuring the fund's investments remain in line with the stated objectives.

Taxation is another key area of compliance. SMSFs have tax obligations, and failure to comply with ATO regulations could result in penalties. Regular audits are also required, and the trustees of the fund are responsible for maintaining accurate financial records.

Now if a retirement plan investment is your end goal for investing, then an SMSF can be one of the best options for you. However, it includes a lot more responsibilities of a typical fund manager which are to be managed by its trustees.

Well to each his own, if someone is comfortable enough to micro-manage it and its advantages are aligned with their future financial goals then it is indeed meant for them.

# Chapter 7

# Protecting Your Wealth by Diversifying Beyond Mutual Funds

Now that we've covered pretty much everything on Mutual Funds. It's time to look at investments beyond these. But wait, is there something wrong with Mutual Funds investment? If not, then why am I referring you to other sorts of Investments. Well, it's your decision on where to invest. But it's my responsibility here to guide you on not just Mutual Funds but other investment opportunities that are currently available in India.
And there's nothing wrong with diversifying your investments.

In fact, diversification is the key to not fully losing your investment value in case of a global financial crisis. As an NRI, diversification provides you with added importance. Although the Indian Stock Market has a rock solid investment base as we discussed in the previous chapters. Fluctuations just like any other stock market still take place. Diversifying beyond stocks plays a major role in keeping your investment safe, in this case.

So here in this chapter, we will discuss other investment opportunities in India and how these can be a game changer for your investment plan.

## Portfolio Management Services (PMS)

Portfolio Management Services (PMS) offer a professional, personalised approach to managing your investments. For people living abroad who may find it challenging to manage their portfolio on their own, PMS can be an excellent solution.

PMS providers take responsibility for building and managing your portfolio, offering a tailor-made investment strategy based on your financial goals, risk tolerance, and time horizon.

## How Does it Work?

A PMS provider will design a unique investment plan tailored specifically to your needs. They have the flexibility to invest in a mix of equities, bonds, mutual funds, and other asset classes. Unlike mutual funds, where the fund manager makes decisions for the entire fund, PMS is more individualised.

You can choose between two types of PMS: discretionary and non-discretionary. In a discretionary PMS, the fund manager has full control over investment decisions. In a non-discretionary PMS, the manager will advise you, but you retain control over the final investment decisions.

So this is how a typical PMS investment works. Let's get to know more about it through some of the benefits it yields.

## Benefits of PMS

**1. The investment that can be Tailored:**

One of the most significant advantages of Portfolio Management Services (PMS) is that it's an investment with a highly personalised nature . Unlike mutual funds, where investments are pooled and managed collectively, PMS tailors a portfolio to the individual investor's needs. This means that every decision made in your portfolio reflects your specific financial goals, risk tolerance, and investment time horizon.

For instance, as an NRI you're looking to invest in India, but you have specific preferences, such as focusing on ethical investments, or avoiding volatile sectors like technology, so accordingly, your PMS manager will design the portfolio around these preferences.

This flexibility is particularly useful for NRIs, who may want to allocate their investments based on the specific conditions of both Indian and international markets. The portfolio is crafted to ensure it aligns perfectly with your financial objectives, whether they are wealth accumulation, regular income, or capital preservation.

## 2. A portfolio that has Active Management:

PMS involves active portfolio management. Unlike traditional mutual funds or even certain passive investment strategies. This means that the PMS manager continuously tracks market trends, economic indicators, and company performance to make timely adjustments to your portfolio.

If the market conditions shift, such as during economic downturns or geopolitical events that impact certain sectors, your portfolio will be adjusted to reflect these changes. For you as NRI, this is particularly important because managing investments from abroad can be challenging.

Time zone differences, limited access to market information, or simply the busy nature of your professional lives can make it difficult to keep up with daily market developments. With PMS, you don't need to constantly monitor your investments, as the manager handles all the work for you, ensuring your portfolio adapts in real-time to market conditions, avoiding losses or capitalising on new opportunities.

## 3. Diversified Multiple Assets:

PMS managers have the flexibility to include a wide variety of assets in your portfolio, which goes beyond the traditional stock and bond allocation. This diversification can include investments in commodities like gold, real estate, alternative investments, and even international markets.

Diversification is a key strategy to mitigate risk, especially for you as an NRI who might want to invest in Indian markets but also spread their investments into global opportunities. For example, in times of stock market volatility, your PMS manager may increase exposure to more stable asset classes like bonds or real estate, ensuring your portfolio remains balanced.

Additionally, commodities such as gold, which have historically been a hedge against inflation and market downturns, could also be included. This ability to invest across multiple asset classes enhances the security of your investments while ensuring opportunities for growth.

**Drawbacks of PMS**

We can't close in on PMS without mentioning some of the drawbacks it might include. Other than its benefits, it does have some drawbacks to it, pretty much like any other investment opportunity. Let me show you these.

## 1. Higher Minimum Investment

One of the primary barriers to entry for PMS is its relatively high minimum investment threshold. Unlike mutual funds, which typically have much lower investment requirements (sometimes as low as ₹500 or ₹1,000 per month for a systematic investment plan), PMS generally requires a minimum investment of ₹50 lakh or more.

This makes PMS a more exclusive investment option, accessible primarily to high-net-worth individuals (HNIs). For NRIs who may not have large sums readily available or are just starting to explore Indian markets, this high entry point could be prohibitive.

In comparison, mutual funds offer more flexibility for small or medium-sized investors who may want to start with a lower capital base and gradually increase their investments over time.

## 2. Management Fees

PMS providers charge management fees for their services, which are generally higher than the fees associated with mutual funds. These fees can range from 1% to 3% of the assets under management, depending on the provider and the services offered.

Additionally, some PMS providers may also charge performance-based fees, meaning they take a percentage of the profits if your portfolio exceeds certain return thresholds. While these fees pay for the expertise and active management provided by the PMS manager, they can eat into your overall returns. For instance, if your portfolio returns 10% in a year but the management fee is 2%, your net return will be reduced to 8%.

Over the long term, these fees can compound and significantly reduce the total returns on your investments, making it a more expensive option compared to mutual funds, where expense ratios are typically much lower (0.5%-2%).

## 3. Market Dependency

While PMS offers a customised and diversified approach to investing, it still remains subject to market risks and fluctuations. The very nature of investing means there is no guaranteed return, and your portfolio's performance will depend on the prevailing market conditions.

For example, if the Indian equity markets are going through a bear phase or are impacted by global economic uncertainties, your PMS portfolio may underperform despite the best efforts of the manager to mitigate risk. Unlike fixed-income products, such as bonds or fixed deposits, PMS does not provide predictable returns. Although the diversification into various asset classes aims to reduce overall risk, it cannot entirely eliminate market-related volatility.

This dependency on market performance may be concerning for conservative investors who prioritise stability over growth, especially for NRIs who may not have regular access to local market updates and prefer a more predictable investment approach.

## Foreign Currency Convertible Bonds (FCCBs)

FCCBs are bonds issued by Indian companies but denominated in foreign currencies, typically US dollars. These bonds combine the characteristics of both debt and equity. As a bondholder, you continue to receive regular interest payments at a fixed rate, but you also have the option to convert the bond into equity shares of the issuing company at a later date.

### Benefits of FCCB

**1. Currency Risk Protection:**

One of the major advantages of Foreign Currency Convertible Bonds (FCCBs) for NRIs is the inherent protection they offer against currency risk. FCCBs are issued in foreign currencies, such as US dollars, euros, or yen, rather than Indian rupees.

This is particularly beneficial for NRIs who earn or hold wealth in foreign currencies, as it helps protect them from fluctuations in the value of the Indian rupee. In markets where the Indian rupee may depreciate over time, FCCBs allow NRIs to avoid the losses that could result from currency devaluation. For example, if the Indian rupee weakens against the US dollar, the value of investments denominated in rupees would decrease when converted back to dollars.

However, since FCCBs are issued in a foreign currency, the principal and interest payments are not impacted by rupee depreciation, providing a safeguard for NRIs who are concerned about currency risks.

## 2. Fixed Income:

FCCBs offer the security of a fixed income stream, providing investors with regular interest payments, typically at a predetermined rate. These interest payments are usually made on a semi-annual or annual basis, offering stability and a reliable source of income for investors.

Even if the issuing company's stock doesn't perform well in the market, you are still entitled to receive the agreed-upon interest payments, which creates a sense of safety and predictability for risk-conscious investors. For NRIs, this fixed income aspect can be particularly valuable because it provides a steady return on investment, regardless of stock market fluctuations.

This is especially beneficial for those looking for stable returns, perhaps to support their families back home or maintain a steady income source while living abroad.

## 3. Potential Equity Upside:

One of the unique features of FCCBs is their dual nature, offering both fixed income and potential capital gains. FCCBs come with an embedded option to convert the bonds into equity shares of the issuing company at a future date, typically at a pre-agreed conversion price.

If the company's stock price appreciates over time, investors have the option to convert their bonds into equity and benefit from the price increase, resulting in potential capital gains. This feature allows NRIs to participate in the upside potential of the company's stock while still enjoying the fixed interest payments associated with bonds.

Essentially, it offers the best of both worlds, fixed income and the opportunity to benefit from equity market growth.

For risk-averse investors, this combination of steady returns with the possibility of capital appreciation makes FCCBs a compelling choice, as it allows them to mitigate risk while still enjoying equity market exposure.

# Risks associated with FCCB

## 1. Conversion Risk:

While the option to convert FCCBs into equity can be an advantage when the company's stock price rises, it also carries a potential downside, conversion risk. If the company's stock does not perform as expected or declines in value, converting the bonds into equity may result in significant losses or reduced returns.

For example, if an investor decides to convert their FCCBs into shares, and the stock price has fallen below the conversion price, the investor may be left holding shares that are worth less than the bond's original value. This can be particularly problematic for NRIs who are counting on the equity conversion as a means of achieving capital gains.

Furthermore, since stock markets can be volatile, there is always the risk that external factors, such as economic downturns, geopolitical events, or changes in the company's financial performance, could negatively impact the stock price, making the conversion option less attractive.

## 2. Credit Risk:

FCCBs are issued by individual companies, meaning that the creditworthiness of the issuing company is a critical factor in assessing the risk of the bond. If the company experiences financial difficulties or mismanagement, there is a risk that it could default on its bond payments, leading to losses for investors.

For NRIs, this is a significant consideration because FCCBs are linked to the financial health of the issuing company. Even if the company initially appears strong, changes in market conditions, increased competition, or internal challenges could weaken its financial standing, increasing the likelihood of default. Additionally, if the company is unable to meet its bond obligations, investors may face delays in receiving interest payments or may lose the principal amount of the bond altogether.

Unlike government bonds, which are backed by the government, FCCBs carry higher credit risk since they are dependent on the company's performance.

## 3. Complexity:

FCCBs can be more complex than traditional bonds or stocks. They require a solid understanding of both fixed-income and equity markets, as well as the timing of bond conversion to equity. For NRIs who may not have the time or expertise to closely monitor these investments, the complexity of FCCBs could pose a challenge.

While they offer a blend of safety and growth potential, it's important to keep in mind the nuanced risks involved with this type of investment.

## Real Estate Investment Trusts (REITs)

Third on our list is REITs. These are companies that own, manage, or finance income-generating real estate. As an investor, you can buy shares in a REIT, just like you would buy shares in a company. REITs typically invest in a portfolio of properties, such as office buildings, shopping centers, or apartments, that generate rental income.

Directly investing in Indian real estate can be difficult for NRIs due to management, legal, and tax challenges. Real Estate Investment Trusts (REITs) offer a way to gain exposure to the real estate market without actually owning property.

### Benefits of REITs (Real Estate Investment Trusts)

**1. Income Generation:**

One of the most appealing benefits of REITs is the reliable income stream they provide. By law, REITs are required to distribute at least 90% of their taxable income to shareholders in the form of dividends. This makes REITs an attractive option for NRIs seeking regular passive income.

Since REITs are typically structured to generate income from leasing, renting, or selling properties, they tend to provide steady cash flow. This feature is especially appealing for retirees or individuals who want a consistent source of income without actively managing properties.

Additionally, REITs tend to yield higher dividends compared to traditional stocks, which makes them an excellent choice for investors who prioritise income generation. NRIs, especially those who may not be in India to manage rental properties or other real estate assets, can benefit from the simplicity of receiving dividend income through REITs without the hassle of property maintenance and management.

## 2. Real Estate Diversification

Another major benefit of investing in REITs is the diversification they offer. When you invest in a REIT, you're not investing in a single property or even a single type of property, but rather a diversified portfolio of real estate assets.

These could range from residential and commercial buildings to hospitals, hotels, or even warehouses and shopping malls. This diversification helps reduce the risks associated with owning a single property.

For example, if one property in the REIT's portfolio underperforms or loses value, the losses are spread across many other properties, mitigating the impact on the investor's overall returns. Moreover, REITs often invest in properties located in different geographical regions.

This geographic diversification can help cushion against localised economic downturns or real estate market slumps in specific areas.

For NRIs, who may be unfamiliar with or unable to manage specific local markets, REITs provide an easy way to gain broad exposure to Indian real estate, without having to invest directly in physical property.

## 3. Convenience of Liquidity

One of the significant drawbacks of direct real estate investment is its illiquidity. Selling a physical property can take months or even years, during which time the market conditions may fluctuate, and the property value could decrease. REITs, on the other hand, provide a high level of liquidity.

Because REIT shares are traded on stock exchanges, they can be bought and sold relatively easily, much like traditional stocks. This feature allows investors to quickly access their funds when needed, without the long wait times typically associated with physical real estate transactions.

For NRIs, this liquidity is invaluable as it allows them to respond to changes in financial needs or market conditions without the complications involved in selling a property abroad.

Moreover, REITs enable investors to take advantage of short-term market opportunities, or divest from real estate without the substantial closing costs or legal hurdles that accompany the sale of a property.

# Drawbacks of REITs

## 1. Management Fees:

Like mutual funds, REITs charge management fees that are used to cover operational expenses and compensate the team managing the real estate assets. These fees are typically a percentage of the REIT's total assets or income and can reduce the investor's overall returns.

While these fees might seem small on paper, over time, they can compound and eat into the returns generated by the REIT. It's essential for NRIs to carefully review the fee structures of any REIT they're considering investing in, as higher fees can significantly impact long-term performance.

Additionally, some REITs charge performance fees, which means that a portion of the gains may go to the managers rather than being passed on to shareholders. For those used to managing their portfolios with low-cost options like exchange-traded funds (ETFs), REITs may appear more expensive in comparison.

However, NRIs must weigh these costs against the benefits, such as professional management and diversification, to determine if REITs align with their investment goals.

## 2. Tax Implications:

Another factor to consider with REITs is the tax treatment of dividends. While REITs offer attractive dividend yields, these dividends are often taxed as ordinary income, rather than at the lower capital gains tax rate, which can reduce the net income that investors receive.

For NRIs, the tax situation can become even more complicated depending on the tax treaties between their country of residence and India. Some countries may tax REIT dividends differently, and there could also be withholding taxes or other cross-border tax considerations that impact the total return on investment.

It's crucial for NRIs to consult with a tax advisor to fully understand how REIT dividends will be taxed in their home country, as well as in India. Proper tax planning is necessary to ensure that the income generated from REIT investments is maximised after accounting for tax liabilities.

## 3. Interest Rate Sensitivity:

Like other income-generating assets, REITs are sensitive to changes in interest rates. When interest rates rise, REITs may become less attractive compared to other fixed-income investments like bonds, which tend to offer higher yields during periods of rising rates. This can cause REIT prices to fall as investors seek higher returns elsewhere.

Additionally, higher interest rates can increase the cost of borrowing for REITs, which can reduce their profitability and lead to lower dividends for shareholders. For NRIs, who may be impacted by both domestic and foreign interest rate environments, it's important to monitor global interest rate trends and their potential impact on REIT performance.

# GIFT City: A New Investment Opportunity

GIFT City is a special economic zone (SEZ) that provides a conducive environment for financial and technological businesses to operate. It offers a variety of investment opportunities, including foreign currency-denominated bonds, derivatives, mutual funds, and even real estate.

The Gujarat International Finance Tec-City (GIFT City) represents a new frontier for NRI investors. It is a global financial hub located in Gujarat, offering a range of tax benefits and investment opportunities, both in Indian and international markets.

## Why Should You as an NRI Invest Through GIFT City?

Well, here are some benefits of great importance that makes it a Golden investment opportunity.

### 1. Tax Benefits of GIFT City:

One of the most significant advantages of investing through the Gujarat International Finance Tec-City (GIFT City) is the range of tax benefits it offers to NRIs. GIFT City has been designated as a Special Economic Zone (SEZ), which allows it to provide various tax exemptions that make it a highly attractive investment destination for global investors.

These tax incentives cover multiple aspects, such as capital gains, interest, and dividend income, creating a powerful opportunity for NRIs to optimise their returns while significantly reducing their tax liabilities.

For instance, capital gains, whether they are short-term or long-term, are usually subject to taxation in most investment avenues. However, GIFT City provides an exemption or reduction in capital gains taxes, depending on the specific investments made. This is particularly beneficial for investors looking to hold assets for extended periods, as it helps maximise the compounded returns on their investments.

In addition to capital gains, the interest earned on investments made through GIFT City is often exempt from tax. This feature can significantly boost the returns for those NRIs who prefer fixed-income securities or other interest-bearing financial instruments.

Given that many NRIs earn interest income from various sources like bonds or savings accounts, this exemption creates a unique advantage for investing through GIFT City over other avenues.

Lastly, the tax exemption on dividends adds another layer of benefit. Dividends are a crucial source of passive income for many investors, and in most jurisdictions, they are taxed as part of regular income. By providing tax relief on dividend income, GIFT City makes it easier for NRIs to generate steady, tax-free income, which can help them accumulate wealth over time.

For NRIs who face high tax rates in their country of residence, the tax incentives available in GIFT City are a great way to legally minimise their overall tax burden, enabling them to maximise their returns without resorting to complex tax-planning strategies.

## 2. Access to Global Markets:

GIFT City is not just about tax savings; it also offers access to a range of global financial markets, allowing NRIs to invest in both Indian and international financial products. This is a unique advantage because it provides investors with the opportunity to diversify their portfolios beyond the Indian market.

Diversification across multiple asset classes and geographies is a fundamental principle of sound investing, and GIFT City allows investors to do exactly that without the usual regulatory hurdles associated with cross-border investments.

For NRIs, access to global markets is crucial as it helps mitigate risks tied to one specific economy or asset class. Indian markets can be volatile, and economic cycles can impact performance.

However, by being able to invest in global markets, NRIs can diversify their investments into more stable or faster-growing economies, depending on their risk tolerance and financial goals. This access opens up opportunities to invest in global equities, bonds, commodities, and even sophisticated derivatives that might not be easily accessible through traditional routes.

Furthermore, GIFT City's framework is designed to encourage participation in innovative financial products, such as derivatives, foreign exchange (forex) trading, and offshore funds, which can offer higher returns for those who are well-versed in these instruments.

For NRIs, particularly those living in financial hubs like Singapore, Dubai, or London, GIFT City's access to global markets can offer a convenient way to blend Indian investments with their existing international portfolios, all under a single platform.

### 3. Regulatory Advantages:

GIFT City is not just about tax savings; it also offers access to a range of global financial markets, allowing NRIs to invest in both Indian and international financial products. This is a unique advantage because it provides investors with the opportunity to diversify their portfolios beyond the Indian market.

Diversification across multiple asset classes and geographies is a fundamental principle of sound investing, and GIFT City allows investors to do exactly that without the usual regulatory hurdles associated with cross-border investments.

For NRIs, access to global markets is crucial as it helps mitigate risks tied to one specific economy or asset class. Indian markets can be volatile, and economic cycles can impact performance.

However, by being able to invest in global markets, NRIs can diversify their investments into more stable or faster-growing economies, depending on their risk tolerance and financial goals.

This access opens up opportunities to invest in global equities, bonds, commodities, and even sophisticated derivatives that might not be easily accessible through traditional routes.

Furthermore, GIFT City's framework is designed to encourage participation in innovative financial products, such as derivatives, foreign exchange (forex) trading, and offshore funds, which can offer higher returns for those who are well-versed in these instruments.

For NRIs, particularly those living in financial hubs like Singapore, Dubai, or London, GIFT City's access to global markets can offer a convenient way to blend Indian investments with their existing international portfolios, all under a single platform.

## Challenges of Investing in GIFT City

Just like any other investment opportunity, this isn't foolproof either. It comes with its own set of challenges. So without being biased, let's talk about these.

## 1. New and Evolving:

Despite its numerous advantages, GIFT City is still a relatively new financial hub, and with that comes certain challenges. One of the primary concerns is that because it is new, many of its policies, procedures, and benefits are still evolving. While the potential is immense, investors must stay informed about ongoing regulatory changes and updates.

For instance, tax benefits or regulatory leniency, which are appealing today, could be subject to changes as the government refines its policies. For NRIs who may not be following Indian financial news as closely, keeping up with these developments can be a challenge.

Moreover, GIFT City does not yet have a long track record. Its relatively short history means that there isn't a significant amount of data on its performance, especially during economic downturns or market disruptions. Investors are taking a leap of faith that the regulatory advantages and tax incentives will continue to be as beneficial in the long run as they appear today.

For those NRIs who are more risk-averse, this lack of historical data may pose a challenge when assessing the long-term viability of investing in GIFT City.

## 2. Infrastructural Challenge

Another potential challenge is the infrastructure. Although GIFT City is rapidly developing, it's still in its early stages. While much of the financial ecosystem is being built to attract global investors, it will take time before all systems are fully operational and functioning at the same efficiency level as more established global financial hubs like Dubai or Singapore.

GIFT City offers a plethora of benefits for NRIs, such as attractive tax incentives, access to global markets, and regulatory advantages, making it a promising investment avenue.

However, as a new financial centre, it comes with its share of challenges, including the evolving nature of its policies and the relatively short track record. Investors must carefully weigh these factors when considering GIFT City as part of their overall investment strategy. While the potential rewards are substantial, it's important to stay informed and adapt to the evolving landscape to fully capitalise on the opportunities that GIFT City presents.

With this piece of information, our chapter comes to an end. In this chapter we learned about various investment opportunities other than Mutual Funds. These investment opportunities can most definitely provide long term benefits, however these come with their own sets of inconveniences, which we also have discussed here.

As always, it's up to you as an investor, what will you choose. After knowing the pros and cons of all types of investments there is in India. And it's my job to let you know every single detail that's possible to include about these. But one thing is clear, no matter which type of investment you choose, you're sure to gain in the long term by investing in the rising superpower we know as India.

# Chapter 8

# Tax Talk: Smooth Sail through Indian and Foreign Taxation as an NRI

Now in this chapter, we will cover the aspect of taxes. A topic that may sound boring but if you want to keep the winnings (your investment gains) intact, without losing a bunch of these unknowingly. Then you definitely need to pay some of your attention here. Although we have talked about these in some aspects in almost every chapter but it's time we learned everything about the Indian taxation system in brief.

What it means for the NRIs and how you can benefit from it while sailing smoothly through these regulations without a hassle in sight.

So, let's start with the basics,

## Who's Considered an NRI When It Comes to Tax Purposes?

As per the Indian Income Tax Act 1961, an Indian person is considered an NRI:

- If they have stayed in India for less than 182 days in a given financial year.

- If they have been outside India for 365 days for the past 4 years and spent less than 60 days in India for the current financial year.

If you meet these criteria, your global income won't be taxed in India. However, your income from Indian sources, such as rent, capital gains, or interest, is taxable.

## Types of Income Taxable in India for NRIs

NRIs are only taxed on income earned in India. Let's break down the key categories:

- **Salary Income**: If you receive a salary for services provided in India, it is taxable.
- **Income from House Property**: Any rental income from properties in India is taxable. NRIs are entitled to the same standard deductions as resident Indians.
- **Capital Gains**: Capital gains from the sale of assets such as property, shares, or mutual funds in India are taxable. The rate depends on the type of asset and the duration for which it was held.
- **Interest Income**: Interest earned from deposits in Indian banks is taxable. Special provisions exist for certain types of accounts, such as the Non-Resident External (NRE) account, where interest is tax-free.
- **Other Sources**: Dividends from shares of Indian companies, winnings from lotteries, or income from other sources within India are also taxable.

## Indian Tax Filing Requirements for NRIs

### When to File Income Tax Returns:

NRIs must file income tax returns in India if:

- Their total income from Indian sources exceeds ₹2.5 lakh in a financial year.
- They have short-term or long-term capital gains from investments in India.
- They wish to claim a tax refund or carry forward losses for future offsetting.

### Documents Needed for Filing

Some key documents required for filing returns in India include:

- PAN card (Permanent Account Number)
- Form 16/16A for salary or pension income
- Bank account statements
- Proof of tax deduction at source (TDS)
- Investment details in shares, mutual funds, or property

## Double Taxation Avoidance Agreements (DTAA)

One of the most important tools in your tax strategy as an NRI is the Double Taxation Avoidance Agreement (DTAA). This is a treaty India has with several countries to prevent NRIs from being taxed on the same income twice.

### What is DTAA?

DTAA is a bilateral agreement between two countries that ensures NRIs don't pay tax on the same income in both countries. India has DTAAs with over 90 countries, including the USA, Australia, UK, Canada, UAE, and Singapore.

## How Does DTAA Work?

There are two primary mechanisms for avoiding double taxation under DTAA:

- **Exemption Method**: The income is taxed in only one country.

- **Tax Credit Method**: The income is taxed in both countries, but the taxpayer gets a credit in their resident country for the tax paid in the source country.

For example, if an NRI earns interest in India and pays tax on it, they can claim a tax credit for the amount paid when filing taxes in their country of residence.

## DTAA Benefits for NRIs:

- **Lower Tax Rates**: DTAAs often provide for lower withholding tax rates on dividends, interest, and royalties.

- **Tax Relief on Services**: Income earned for services rendered in one country but paid in another may enjoy tax relief.

- **Clarity on Capital Gains**: Certain DTAAs provide clarity on how capital gains from the sale of assets will be taxed.

## Strategic Investments and Tax Planning

With the right planning, NRIs can significantly reduce their tax liabilities and keep more of their earnings.

## Choosing Tax-Efficient Investments:

Tax planning starts with selecting the right investment vehicles:

- **NRE and FCNR Accounts**: Interest on these accounts is exempt from tax in India, making them ideal for NRIs.

- **Capital Gains from Mutual Funds**: Long-term capital gains (LTCG) on equity mutual funds are exempt up to ₹1 lakh annually. Gains exceeding this amount are taxed at 10%, while short-term capital gains (STCG) are taxed at 15%.

- **Fixed Deposits**: Unlike NRE accounts, interest on Non-Resident Ordinary (NRO) fixed deposits is taxable. However, it can be a good option for NRIs wanting to repatriate funds.

**Deductions and Exemptions:**

Just like resident Indians, NRIs can take advantage of various deductions under Indian tax laws:

- **Section 80C**: NRIs can claim deductions of up to ₹1.5 lakh on investments like life insurance premiums, provident fund contributions, and ELSS (Equity-Linked Savings Scheme) funds.

- **Home Loan Deductions**: NRIs can claim deductions on the interest paid on home loans under Section 24, as well as principal repayment under Section 80C.

- **Health Insurance**: Premiums paid for health insurance under Section 80D are deductible, with limits depending on the age of the insured.

- **Education Loan**: Interest paid on an education loan for higher studies is eligible for deduction under Section 80E without any upper limit.

**Tax on Real Estate Investments**

Real estate is a popular investment choice for NRIs, but it comes with specific tax implications:

- **Rental Income**: Rental income from property is taxed as per the NRI's income tax slab.

- **Property Sale**: The sale of property attracts capital gains tax. If the property is sold within two years of purchase, it is considered a short-term capital gain, while sales after two years fall under long-term capital gains, with a tax rate of 20% after indexation benefits.

- **Repatriation of Sale Proceeds**: NRIs can repatriate the proceeds of property sales after paying the applicable taxes, and repatriation up to $1 million per financial year is allowed under FEMA (Foreign Exchange Management Act) regulations.

**Foreign Tax Obligations for NRIs**

While managing Indian taxes, NRIs also need to consider their tax obligations in their country of residence. Here's how they can manage taxation on global income.

## Understanding Foreign Tax Systems:

The tax systems in most countries follow either a residence-based or a source-based taxation model. In residence-based systems, global income is taxable in the country where the individual resides. In source-based systems, only income earned within that country is taxable.

## Filing Tax Returns in Foreign Countries:

Most countries require NRIs to declare their global income. If you are an NRI living in a country with a residence-based tax system like the USA, your worldwide income, including what you earn in India, must be declared.

## Foreign Tax Credits:

To avoid double taxation, many countries offer foreign tax credits for taxes paid in another country. For example, an NRI residing in the USA can claim a tax credit for taxes paid on Indian income, ensuring they don't pay tax twice.

## Tax Implications of Repatriating Funds to India

Repatriation of funds by NRIs involves moving money back to India, whether for investment or personal reasons. The Indian government has made this process relatively easy, but there are still some tax implications.

## NRE and NRO Accounts for Repatriation:

- **NRE Accounts**: Funds in NRE accounts, including interest, are fully repatriable, and both the principal and interest are tax-free.

- **NRO Accounts**: Funds in NRO accounts are subject to Indian taxes, and repatriation is limited to $1 million per financial year.

## Tax on Foreign Remittances:

Funds remitted from abroad to India are not taxed in India, provided they are transferred to an NRE account. However, NRIs should check the tax regulations in their resident country, as some jurisdictions might consider these transfers taxable.

## Avoiding Common Tax Pitfalls

**Lack of Awareness of Resident Status:**

One of the most common mistakes is not being aware of your tax residency status. A prolonged stay in India could inadvertently shift your tax status from NRI to resident, changing your tax liabilities.

**Ignoring DTAA Benefits:**

Failing to take advantage of DTAA benefits can result in unnecessary tax payments. NRIs should ensure they claim tax relief on eligible income by providing the necessary documents, such as a Tax Residency Certificate (TRC). (a document issued by the Income Tax department of a taxpayer's resident country in order to prove an individual's residence in that nation for a particular financial year.)

**Not Maintaining Proper Records:**

Maintaining records of income, investments, and tax filings in both India and your country of residence is essential for smooth tax management and avoiding penalties.

So, this wasn't so hard to grasp now right? Now these are the only things you need to keep in mind as an NRI to save yourself from any kind of trouble with respect to following the tax structure in India. In this chapter, you've learned about how to be compliant with the Indian tax structure as well as essential tax saving methods that can help you get the most out of your investment in the long run.

# Chapter 9

# Tapping into the Future of India's Emerging Sectors

In this chapter, we will discuss about the investment opportunities in the emerging sectors of India. Although the accurate future can't be predicted by anyone, the least of all economists making these analyses. But looking at the current growth and technological advancements taking place in every corner of the country, it's safe to say the future of tech savvy advancements doesn't look bleak.

And with these modern advancements come investment opportunities which we will discuss here in this chapter, so stay tuned. Because who knows, if this little piece of information could be your next life changing investment.

So without further ado, let's discuss these emerging sectors shaping the future of the Indian economy.

## Renewable Energy: Powering the Future

India has been constantly putting pressure on transitioning towards clean and renewable energy sources. As a result, the government has set ambitious targets to reduce its carbon footprint, with plans to generate 500 GW of renewable energy by 2030.

Solar and wind energy, in particular, are at the forefront of this revolution, which is driven by government incentives and a growing push for sustainability.

### What's driving its Growth?

- **Government Policies:** Initiatives such as the National Solar Mission and various subsidies are encouraging investments in solar power projects. Wind energy also benefits from tax incentives, making it an attractive investment.

- **Global Demand for Sustainability:** The global shift towards green energy is pushing India to become a key player in the renewable energy sector.

- **Technological Advancements:** Improvements in energy storage solutions, such as batteries, are making renewable energy more reliable and scalable.

### How the NRIs Can Take Advantage of such an opportunity to Invest in this Sector?

You as an NRI can successfully invest in this opportunity of the future via these 3 methods:

- **Green Mutual Funds:** Several Indian mutual funds focus on clean energy sectors, including companies involved in renewable energy production, energy-efficient solutions, and sustainable infrastructure.

- **Infrastructure Investment Trusts (InvITs):** These are relatively new in the Indian market but offer NRIs an opportunity to invest in infrastructure projects, including renewable energy.

- **Direct Equity Investments:** Many Indian companies in the renewable energy space are publicly listed, allowing NRIs to invest directly in their growth story.

## Technology and Innovation: Driving India's Digital Transformation

India's technology sector has always been one of its strongest performers, and with the ongoing digital revolution, the opportunities are only expanding. Apart from being famous for its IT industry, India is now also leading in other futuristic sectors from fintech to artificial intelligence (AI), blockchain, and cloud computing. Looks like India is indeed at the forefront of technological innovation.

## What's driving the growth of this sector?

- **Government Push for Digital India**: The Digital India initiative is creating a massive demand for digital infrastructure, cybersecurity, and data-driven solutions.
- **Rising Consumer Adoption**: With more than 700 million internet users and growing, India is one of the largest digital consumer markets in the world. This translates into opportunities in e-commerce, digital payments, and online services.
- **Startup Ecosystem**: India has become the third-largest startup ecosystem globally, with a thriving community of tech entrepreneurs and innovators.

## How the NRIs Can Invest in this Growth Opportunity?

- **Tech-Focused Mutual Funds**: Several mutual funds in India are geared toward investing in the technology sector, particularly in companies that are part of the digital transformation journey.
- **Venture Capital and Private Equity**: For NRIs with a higher risk appetite, investing in tech startups through venture capital or private equity funds can be a lucrative option. Many funds focus specifically on India's rapidly evolving startup landscape.
- **Direct Equity**: Publicly listed tech companies, such as Infosys, TCS, and Wipro, have been consistent performers and are expanding into newer tech domains such as AI, big data, and cloud services.

## Healthcare and Pharmaceuticals: The Global Medical Hub

As of today, India is the leading hub for medical tourism worldwide. People from all parts of the world visit India for their medical treatments. Primarily due to its biggest pool of brilliant Doctors worldwide and its cost efficient treatments.

India is also one of the largest producers of generic drugs globally and is fast becoming a hub for healthcare innovation. The country's healthcare sector is expected to grow significantly in the coming decade, driven by increasing healthcare needs, medical tourism, and the government's focus on healthcare infrastructure.

## What's Driving Growth in this Sector?

- **Rising Demand**: India's population is ageing, and there's increasing demand for healthcare services, from hospital care to diagnostic services and pharmaceuticals.
- **Medical Tourism**: India is a preferred destination for medical tourism, given its quality healthcare services at relatively low costs. This trend is expected to grow as more international patients seek affordable medical treatments.
- **Government Initiatives**: The government's focus on expanding healthcare infrastructure through programs such as Ayushman Bharat is driving investments in the sector.

## How the NRIs Can Invest in this Growth Driven Sector?

- **Healthcare and Pharma Mutual Funds**: NRIs can invest in mutual funds focused on the healthcare sector. These funds typically invest in pharmaceutical companies, hospital chains, and diagnostic firms.
- **Direct Equity in Pharma Companies**: Many of India's pharmaceutical companies, such as Sun Pharma and Dr. Reddy's Laboratories, are global leaders in generic drugs and biotechnology. Investing in these companies offers exposure to the global healthcare market.
- **Real Estate Investment in Healthcare**: NRIs can also explore investing in healthcare-related real estate, such as hospitals and healthcare facilities, which are expected to grow in demand.

# Infrastructure: Building India's Future

India's infrastructure sector is at the core of its development strategy. In the past decade, India has created several records to its name primarily in the infrastructure sector. For eg. - Completing an expressway in the shortest given time worldwide or completing a 100 km road in just 100 hrs. Creating a world record.

And all of this is possible due to the government's heavy investment in infrastructure such as building roads, railways, airports, and urban infrastructure to support economic growth. This makes infrastructure one of the most promising sectors for long-term investment.

## What's Driving Growth in this Sector?

- **Government Initiatives**: Programs such as the National Infrastructure Pipeline (NIP) and the Smart Cities Mission are designed to modernise India's infrastructure, creating vast opportunities for investment.
- **Urbanisation**: India is rapidly urbanising, with millions of people migrating to cities each year. This is driving demand for housing, transportation, and utilities.
- **Public-Private Partnerships (PPPs)**: Many infrastructure projects are being executed through PPP models, where private investors can participate in the development and operation of these projects.

## How the NRIs Can Invest in this Sector:

- **Infrastructure Mutual Funds**: Several mutual funds invest in companies involved in infrastructure development, including construction, power, and transport sectors.
- **Real Estate Investment Trusts (REITs)**: NRIs can invest in REITs, which allow individuals to invest in income-generating real estate assets, such as commercial properties and infrastructure projects.
- **Direct Investment in Infrastructure Stocks**: Many infrastructure companies, such as Larsen & Toubro and GMR Infrastructure, are publicly listed and offer NRIs a way to invest directly in the sector.

# Financial Services: The Growth of Fintech and Banking

Due to tremendous GDP growth over the past decade. Indian Financial Sector has undergone tremendous transformation. Which is primarily driven by the rise of fintech companies, digital payments and expandin g access to financial services. Currently, millions of Indians are yet to avail access to such services so there's a scope for further record breaking growth in this sector.

## What's Driving Growth in this Sector?

- **Revolution of Fintech:** India is currently witnessing a fintech boom as the new age start-ups are now offering innovative financial services such as digital payments, peer to peer lending and robo advisory platforms.

  - **Inclusion of Fintech:** The Indian Govt.'s push for financial institutions with the inclusion of programs such as Pradhan Mantri Dhan Jan Yojana, that is aimed at bringing millions of people into the banking system.

  - **Rising Disposable Income:** With the growth of middle class population, the growth of financial services, insurance and wealth management is imminent.

## How the NRIs can Invest in this Sector?

- **Fintech Mutual Funds:** Some mutual funds are focused on fintech companies and digital payment platforms, offering you as an NRI a way to invest in this high-growth sector.

- **Banking and Financial Services Stocks:** NRIs can invest directly in leading banks and financial institutions, such as HDFC Bank, ICICI Bank, and Axis Bank, which are expanding into digital services.

- **Digital Payment Companies:** With the growth of digital payments in India, companies like Paytm and PhonePe are attracting significant investor interest. NRIs can explore investment opportunities in these fintech companies as they prepare for potential public listings.

## Electric Vehicles (EVs) and the Automobile Industry

India's automobile industry is undergoing a massive transformation, with a strong push towards electric vehicles (EVs). The leading companies in this sector are Tata Group, Mahindra Group and OLA (for 2 wheelers). The government's focus on reducing carbon emissions and promoting sustainable transportation is driving growth in this sector.

## What's Driving Growth in this Sector?

- **Government Incentives**: Subsidies and incentives for EV manufacturers and buyers are making electric vehicles more affordable and attractive.

- **Rising Environmental Awareness**: As concerns about pollution and climate change grow, more consumers are shifting towards environmentally friendly transportation options.

- **Technological Innovations**: Advances in battery technology and EV infrastructure are making electric vehicles a viable alternative to traditional combustion engine cars.

## How the NRIs can Invest in this Sector?

- **EV-Focused Mutual Funds**: NRIs can invest in mutual funds that focus on companies involved in the production of electric vehicles, battery technology, and charging infrastructure.

- **Automobile Stocks**: Leading Indian automobile manufacturers, such as Tata Motors and Mahindra & Mahindra, are investing heavily in electric vehicles and offer potential for long-term growth.

So these are your best prospects related to the future of investments in India. These industries align with the global emerging trends and India with one of the most skilled workforce, Govt.'s push for these sectors and one of the youngest populations on the planet that makes up for a large consumer base, is set for a remarkable growth that has been previously only associated with China. Perhaps, with the right push, it could even exceed the expectations.

Whether it exceeds the expectations in terms of growth or performs a bit below the expectation. In both cases, you as an NRI can expect much better returns by investing in India than elsewhere.

# Chapter 10

# A Guide to Retirement and Investment Options

Well, so far we've discussed about How to invest in Mutual Funds and the tax structure of India and other investment opportunities. Now comes the part where we seek info about retirement plans for NRIs that India has to offer. Yes, you may forget about your country but your country won't forget about you, so it has come up with retirement benefits to keep you attached to it somehow just like a citizen.

Now retirement planning is not just about building a financial corpus for your non-working years. It is also about making sure that your money grows efficiently, with respect to considering inflation and the lifestyle you want to maintain. As an NRI, your global income, tax residency status, and investment opportunities all affect your retirement strategy.

So let's discuss further into this topic, so this knowledge could help you save a fortune for your retirement. Key considerations you should include here:

- Ensuring a stable income stream during retirement.
- Protecting your corpus against inflation and currency fluctuations.
- Maximising tax benefits on your investments in India and abroad.

The earlier you start planning, the more time you have to benefit from the power of compounding and make informed adjustments to your investment strategy. As we discussed in the previous chapters.

## Understanding Pension Schemes for NRIs

India offers several pension schemes that you as NRI can participate in to create a reliable income stream during their retirement years. These schemes are primarily aimed at individuals looking to secure long-term financial stability.

# 1. National Pension System (NPS)

The National Pension System (NPS) is a voluntary, government-backed pension scheme open to Indian citizens, including the NRIs. The NPS allows you to contribute regularly throughout your working life, and at the time of your retirement, a portion of your savings can be withdrawn, while the rest must be used to buy an annuity to provide a steady income post-retirement.

Its Key Features Includes:

- **Eligibility**: NRIs between the ages of 18 to 70 years can open an NPS account.

- **Investment Options**: Subscribers can choose between different asset classes like equity, corporate bonds, and government securities, offering flexibility to manage risk.

- **Tax Benefits**: Contributions made under NPS are eligible for tax deductions under Section 80C and Section 80CCD of the Income Tax Act.

- **Withdrawal**: Upon reaching the age of 60, you can withdraw up to 60% of the corpus, and the remaining 40% must be used to purchase an annuity.

Advantages for NRIs:

- NPS provides a long-term, low-cost investment opportunity.
- Tax efficiency, with the ability to claim deductions and exemptions under Indian tax laws.
- Flexibility in investment choice and asset allocation.

Challenges that come with it:

- Currency risks may affect the overall return if your retirement is outside India.
- The annuity payments are taxable as per Indian laws, which may not be advantageous depending on the tax treaty between India and your country of residence. (Kindly check the same before initiating this retirement plan)

# 2. Employee Provident Fund (EPF)

The Employee Provident Fund (EPF) is another retirement savings option for NRIs who previously worked in India and contributed to this scheme. Under the EPF, both employer and employee contribute to a retirement corpus, which earns a fixed interest rate.

**Key Features Includes:**

- NRIs can maintain their EPF accounts even after moving abroad, and they can continue to earn interest on the corpus.

- Upon retirement or when no longer employed in India, NRIs can withdraw the entire accumulated amount.

- EPF is considered a relatively low-risk investment, with guaranteed returns.

**Tax Benefits:**

- Interest earned on the EPF account is tax-free in India, but it may be taxable in your country of residence depending on local laws.

- Withdrawals after a continuous service of five years are tax-free.

## 3. Annuities as a Reliable Retirement Income

Annuities are financial products that provide a steady stream of income, typically for life, in exchange for a lump sum investment. For NRIs, annuities can be an excellent tool to ensure a stable post-retirement income.

**Types of Annuities**

There are various types of annuities available in the market, and understanding them is key to making an informed decision:

1. **Immediate Annuities**: In this type, the annuity payments begin almost immediately after you make a lump sum investment. This is suitable for NRIs nearing retirement age and looking for a stable income source.

2. **Deferred Annuities**: In a deferred annuity plan, the payments start after a certain period. This option is better suited for younger NRIs who wish to accumulate a larger corpus over time and then start receiving a regular income at retirement.

3. **Fixed vs. Variable Annuities**: Fixed annuities offer a guaranteed payout, providing peace of mind but often at a lower return. Variable annuities, on the other hand, allow you to invest in market-linked instruments, which can offer higher returns but come with greater risk.

**Advantages of Annuities for NRIs**:

- Provides a stable and reliable income stream during retirement.
- Annuities in India often offer the flexibility to receive payments in the local currency of your country of residence.
- Some annuities also provide death benefits, ensuring your dependents are taken care of in your absence.

**Challenges that come with it:**

- Annuity returns may be lower compared to other market-linked retirement investments.
- Taxation on annuity payments can vary based on tax residency and double taxation agreements between India and the NRI's country of residence.

## 4. Systematic Investment Plans (SIPs) for Retirement Planning

Systematic Investment Plans (SIPs) are a popular way for NRIs to accumulate wealth over time, with relatively lower risk compared to lump-sum investments. SIPs allow you to invest a fixed amount of money at regular intervals, usually in mutual funds, helping you create a substantial retirement corpus gradually.

Since we've already learned about how SIPs work in the previous chapters, so we'll skip that part.

### SIP as a Wealth Building Tool for NRIs

For NRIs, SIPs provide a disciplined approach to retirement planning. The key benefits include:

- **Affordability**: With SIPs, you don't need a large sum to start investing. NRIs can begin SIPs with as little as INR 500 per month.
- **Flexibility**: You can pause, increase, or decrease your SIPs based on your financial situation.
- **Power of Compounding**: As you remain invested over a long period, the compounding effect on your investments can significantly grow your wealth.

### Choosing the Right SIP for Retirement

Although we've also discussed this earlier but just to jog your memory here it again. When selecting a mutual fund for your SIP, consider the following:

- **Risk Appetite**: Equity mutual funds are riskier but offer higher returns, making them suitable for younger NRIs with a longer time horizon. Debt mutual funds, while safer, provide lower returns and are more suited for those nearing retirement.

- **Fund Performance**: Always evaluate the historical performance of the fund. However, past performance should not be the only criterion, look at fund management and consistency in returns.

- **Tax Efficiency**: Some funds provide better tax advantages for NRIs, such as equity-linked savings schemes (ELSS), which qualify for tax deductions under Section 80C.

## Tax Implications of Retirement Investments for NRIs

Taxation is a significant factor NRIs must consider while planning retirement investments. As each country has different tax rules, so you as an NRI need to be aware of how your investments in India are taxed and whether any double taxation treaties apply.

### Double Taxation Avoidance Agreements (DTAA)

As we learned about DTAA in the previous chapters, India has signed Double Taxation Avoidance Agreements (DTAA) with several countries, which ensure that NRIs do not have to pay tax twice on the same income, once in India and again in their country of residence.

So, if you're investing in pension plans, annuities, or mutual funds in India, it's essential to consult a tax advisor to understand how these treaties can help you reduce your overall tax liability.

### Tax Benefits for Retirement Investments

Different retirement investment options come with various tax benefits:

- **NPS**: Tax deductions on contributions are available under Section 80C, and additional benefits can be claimed under Section 80CCD(1B).

- **SIPs**: Equity mutual funds are subject to long-term capital gains tax (LTCG) of 10% on gains above INR 1 lakh after one year, while debt funds are subject to LTCG at 20% after indexation for holdings above three years.

- **Annuities**: The annuity payments are taxable as income in India, and taxation abroad will depend on the tax treaty.

So there you go folks, that's all you needed to know about retirement plans that the Indian government has in store for you. Of course, each plan is designed differently for individuals based on their risk appetite and the nature of investment they choose. And if you do choose to pick one of these, make sure to cross-check info such as taxation rules that India might have with your country (DTAA) and weigh in pros and cons of these to see which one suits you the best.

I have guided you on these, now you're equipped with the right amount of knowledge to make the decision of choosing the retirement plan for your future self.

# Chapter 11

# Creating Wealth that Lasts for Generations to Come

If there's one Indian thing you can't take out of an Indian is our pertinent preference to save for our future generations. It has been the same since forever. Your great grandfather left it for your grandad and your dad, while your grandad and dad will do the same for you. And this sort of tradition isn't going away any time soon.

So, this chapter is all about strategies one needs to enact and the mindset one should develop to create a legacy of wealth for your future generations.

## The Concept of Generational Wealth

Generational wealth as we know in simple terms refers to the assets passed down from one generation to the next. This can include cash savings, investments, property, and businesses. For many, the goal of creating generational wealth is to ensure that their descendants are financially secure and have opportunities for education, career development, and a comfortable life. However, it is not just about passing on money; it's about passing on values, habits, and a mindset that encourages the continued growth and protection of that wealth.

## Mindset Shift: From Individual Success to Legacy Building

It's all in the mindset. To create wealth for the next generations, the one thing that you should focus on is shifting your mindset from the goals of individual success to an ambition of legacy building. Rather than focusing solely on your own financial security, consider how your actions today will impact the financial well-being of your family in the future.

This requires a long-term vision and disciplined financial habits that prioritise sustainable wealth growth over quick gains.

These Key aspects of the mindset shift include:

1. **Thinking Beyond Your Lifetime**: Building generational wealth requires planning that extends beyond your lifetime. Consider how your investments, savings, and financial decisions today will benefit your children, grandchildren, and even great-grandchildren.
2. **Instilling Financial Literacy**: Generational wealth can easily be eroded if future generations are not equipped with the knowledge and skills to manage it. A crucial part of legacy building is ensuring that your family is financially literate and understands how to preserve and grow the wealth you pass on.
3. **Emphasising Long-Term Goals**: While short-term gains can be tempting, wealth that endures is built on long-term goals and stable investments. Prioritise strategies that focus on steady growth, diversification, and risk management to safeguard your wealth.

## Key Strategies for Creating Generational Wealth

These are some simple to follow but crucial aspects without which your journey to building wealth is incomplete.

## 1. Invest in Assets that Appreciate Over Time

The foundation of generational wealth lies in acquiring assets that appreciate over time, such as real estate, stocks, bonds, and businesses. These assets not only provide income during your lifetime but also grow in value, ensuring that future generations inherit a solid financial base.

- **Real Estate**: Property is a tangible asset that has historically appreciated in value over time. For NRIs, investing in real estate in India or abroad can be a powerful way to build long-term wealth. Consider properties in growing markets where the potential for value appreciation is high. Rental income from property can also serve as a steady source of cash flow for generations.

- **Stock Market Investments**: Equities, when invested wisely, offer substantial returns over the long term. Through diversified mutual funds, blue-chip stocks, or exchange-traded funds (ETFs), NRIs can take advantage of global and Indian market growth. For creating generational wealth, focus on long-term stock investments that benefit from compounding returns and reinvestment of dividends.

- **Business Ownership**: Building or investing in businesses can offer exponential growth opportunities. If you are an entrepreneur, your business could be passed down to future generations as a source of income and prosperity. If entrepreneurship isn't your path, consider investing in well-established companies with strong growth potential.

## 2. Leverage Compounding Through SIPs and Long-Term Investments

The power of compounding is one of the most effective tools for wealth creation. As discussed in previous chapters, Systematic Investment Plans (SIPs) allow you to invest small amounts regularly in mutual funds, and over time, these investments grow as both the capital and the returns earn interest.

For creating generational wealth, consistency is key. By starting SIPs early and maintaining them over decades, you can accumulate a significant corpus that not only benefits you but also provides a financial foundation for future generations.

## 3. Establish a Trust or Family Office

For high-net-worth individuals, setting up a family trust or office can be an effective way to manage and protect wealth across generations.

- **Family Trusts**: A trust is a legal structure that holds and manages assets on behalf of beneficiaries. By establishing a family trust, you can ensure that your wealth is distributed according to your wishes while minimizing estate taxes. Trusts can also protect assets from being mismanaged by future generations who may not yet have the financial acumen to handle large sums of money.

- **Family Offices**: A family office is a private wealth management firm dedicated to managing the financial and investment needs of a family. For NRIs with significant wealth, a family office can provide customized solutions for wealth preservation, tax planning, and investment management, ensuring that your wealth continues to grow for future generations.

## 4. Diversify Your Investments

Diversification is a critical strategy for protecting and growing wealth over the long term. By spreading investments across different asset classes, such as stocks, bonds, real estate, and commodities, you can reduce risk and increase the likelihood of stable returns.

As an NRI you should consider both domestic and international investment opportunities to benefit from global growth while safeguarding against localised market downturns.

## 5. Inheritance and Estate Planning

Proper estate planning ensures that your wealth is transferred to your heirs in the most efficient and tax-effective manner. Without a proper plan, a significant portion of your wealth could be lost to taxes or legal disputes.

- **Will and Testament**: Ensure that you have a clear and legally binding will that outlines how your assets will be distributed. This can prevent conflicts among heirs and ensure that your wishes are followed.

- **Nomination in Investments**: NRIs should ensure that they have appointed nominees for all investments, including mutual funds, bank accounts, and insurance policies. Nomination allows for the smooth transfer of assets to the designated person without going through the lengthy legal process.

- **Tax Planning**: Different countries have varying tax rules regarding inheritance. NRIs should be aware of the inheritance tax laws in their country of residence and in India. Effective tax planning can help minimise the tax burden on future generations.

# Passing Down Financial Knowledge and Values

Wealth that lasts is not just about money, it is about imparting the values and knowledge needed to maintain and grow that wealth as our parents did for us and their parents did for them. Because there's no amount of wealth that can last forever if the bearer of the wealth isn't equipped with the right knowledge to maintain it.

So it gets even more important to educate your family about financial management, responsible spending, and the importance of long-term planning is essential to ensuring that your financial legacy is preserved.

## 1. Financial Literacy for Future Generations

Ensure that your children and grandchildren are educated about financial matters. Teach them the importance of saving, investing, and responsible money management. Encourage them to take an interest in family finances and involve them in discussions about wealth creation and preservation.

## 2. Inculcate a Culture of Investment

Create a family culture that values investing and financial responsibility. By exposing younger generations to the principles of investing early on, you can instill a mindset of wealth creation that will benefit them throughout their lives.

## 3. Create a Family Financial Mission Statement

Some families choose to create a financial mission statement, a set of guiding principles that outline how the family views wealth, its responsibilities, and its future. This can serve as a blueprint for how future generations should handle their inheritance, ensuring that the family wealth is used wisely and preserved for as long as possible.

Vision to see ahead in the future, and discipline to follow your long term approach to financial management are needed for building a legacy of generational wealth. You've now been educated with various investment opportunities but what's even more important is passing down this financial knowledge and instilling a culture of responsible wealth management. And this way you can definitely make sure the wealth that you worked hard for, will be preserved for generations to come.

It's a journey that begins today, but its impact will be felt for years, if not centuries, to come.

# Chapter 12

# Success Stories of the NRI Investors

This chapter will cover the real life success stories of NRI investors who have reaped the benefits by investing early, gaining insights into the framework of investment opportunities in India, leveraging the power of SIPs and compounding have successfully achieved praise worthy gains on their investments.

I will talk about the approach and the outcome of the investment of these NRIs made in India. And what you can learn from them.

## 1. Case Study One: Shailesh Sood's Strategic SIP Journey - Compounding Wealth Over Time

Shailesh Sood, an NRI based in the United States, had always been mindful of his finances but was unsure about how to leverage the Indian market for long-term wealth creation. His primary focus was building a retirement corpus, and like many others, he feared market volatility.

However, a conversation with a financial advisor back in 2010 introduced him to the idea of Systematic Investment Plans (SIPs) in India.

**Shailesh's Approach:**

His goal was simple, to invest in mutual funds through SIPs and allow the power of compounding to work its magic over time. He began by investing ₹10,000 per month into a mix of equity and hybrid funds that catered to both high-growth potential and moderate-risk exposure.

- **Why SIPs?** Shailesh was attracted to SIPs because of the rupee-cost averaging and the flexibility to invest small amounts regularly, which helped him avoid timing the market.

- **The Power of Compounding**: Over 12 years, his consistent investments began to show impressive growth. The combination of his monthly contributions and the compounding effect of his returns saw his corpus steadily increase.

## The Outcome:

By 2022, Shailesh's total investment of ₹14.4 lakh had grown to over ₹60 lakh, thanks to the market's upward trajectory and the power of compounding. Shailesh continues his SIP journey with increased contributions, confident that this long-term approach will provide him with a comfortable retirement corpus. He also plans to use a portion of these funds to support his children's education in the future.

## What You Can Learn from it:

This story highlights how disciplined investing over the long term, even with modest contributions, can lead to substantial wealth creation. His experience serves as a reminder to many NRIs that SIPs are a powerful tool for building wealth over time without needing to worry about daily market fluctuations.

## Case Study 2: Sunita's Real Estate Success – Investing in India's Property Boom

Sunita Patil, an NRI living in Dubai, always had an affinity for real estate but wasn't sure if investing in India would yield the returns she hoped for. In 2013, after watching India's real estate market grow, Sunita decided to take a leap of faith and purchase property in Gurugram, one of India's fastest-growing cities.

## Sunita's Approach:

She carefully researched emerging real estate markets in India, focusing on cities with high demand for housing due to their growing IT sectors and infrastructure development. Gurugram stood out due to its strong economy, influx of skilled professionals, and high demand for residential properties.

- **Location**: Sunita chose a pre-launch project in an upcoming neighbourhood close to Gurugram's IT corridor. She knew that proximity to workplaces, schools, and hospitals would drive demand and price appreciation.

- **Risk Mitigation**: To mitigate the risks of investing in a pre-launch project, Sunita thoroughly vetted the developer, ensuring they had a strong track record of timely delivery and high-quality construction.

## The Outcome:

By 2020, Sunita's investment had appreciated by nearly 170%, far exceeding her expectations. Her property, initially purchased for ₹80 lakh, was now valued at ₹2.16 crore. Additionally, she had rented out the property to professionals working in Gurugram's IT sector, securing a consistent rental income that covered her loan repayments and provided extra cash flow.

## What You Can Learn from it:

Her success story underscores the importance of timing and research in real estate investing. By choosing a fast-developing area and carefully vetting her investment, she was able to capitalise on India's booming property market. Sunita is now exploring further real estate opportunities in other emerging Indian cities, confident in the strength of the market.

## Case Study 3: Rahul's Early Investment in Indian Startups – Tapping Into India's Tech Revolution

Rahul Verma, a UK-based NRI, always had an entrepreneurial spirit. He was closely following India's burgeoning startup ecosystem and saw immense potential in its tech-driven future. In 2015, after reading about government initiatives such as Startup India and the rise of innovative Indian startups, Rahul decided to diversify his investments by participating in early-stage funding rounds for Indian tech companies.

**Rahul's Approach:**

Rahul had a strong background in technology and understood the startup landscape well. He began by networking with Indian founders and venture capitalists, identifying promising startups in the fields of fintech, e-commerce, and SaaS (Software as a Service).

- **Diversified Portfolio**: Instead of putting all his money into one company, Rahul diversified his investments across several startups, understanding that startup investments are high-risk but can offer incredible returns.

- **Long-Term Vision**: Rahul was not seeking immediate returns but was willing to wait 5-10 years for his investments to mature. He believed in the potential of these startups to disrupt industries and scale rapidly in India's growing economy.

**The Outcome:**

Rahul's patience paid off. By 2022, two of the startups he invested in had become unicorns (companies valued at over $1 billion). His ₹20 lakh initial investment in these startups grew exponentially, providing him with returns of over ₹5 crore.

Rahul continues to stay involved with India's startup ecosystem, reinvesting his gains and providing mentorship to new founders.

**What You Can Learn from it:**

Rahul's story is a testament to the potential of India's tech revolution. By being an early investor in promising startups, he not only achieved significant financial success but also played a part in shaping the future of India's innovation landscape. His strategic risk-taking and understanding of the startup world allowed him to tap into a rapidly growing sector.

## Key Takeaways from NRI Success Stories

Now here are some takeaways we can learn from the case studies of these successful investors.

1. **Long-Term Thinking**: Whether through SIPs, real estate, or startups, all three investors demonstrated the power of long-term thinking. They were patient, strategic, and willing to wait for their investments to mature, reaping significant rewards as a result.

2. **Diversification**: Spreading investments across different sectors and asset classes helped these investors mitigate risks and ensure consistent growth. Shailesh diversified through mutual funds, Sunita through real estate, and Rahul through startups, each achieving success in their respective fields.

3. **Research and Timing**: Understanding the market, timing the investment well, and conducting thorough research played a crucial role in the success of each case study. Sunita's research into the real estate market, Rahul's networking in the startup community, and Shailesh's consultation with financial experts all contributed to their achievements.

4. **The Power of Compounding**: Shailesh's SIP journey emphasises how small, consistent investments can lead to substantial growth through the power of compounding. For NRIs looking to build wealth steadily, SIPs offer a low-risk, high-reward opportunity.

5. **Opportunities in India's Growth Story**: Each investor capitalised on India's rapid economic growth, whether through its real estate boom, booming tech startups, or thriving stock market. NRIs can benefit immensely by staying connected to India's growth trajectory and seizing opportunities in emerging markets and sectors.

# The Conclusion

The world of mutual funds is vast and full of opportunities, and as an NRI, you are in a particularly advantageous position to tap into both global and Indian markets. This dual exposure allows you to diversify your investments in ways that few others can, balancing your portfolio across geographies and asset classes.

Whether it's the booming Indian economy or stable international markets, you have access to a broad range of opportunities that can help you achieve both your short-term financial goals and long-term wealth aspirations. Mutual funds offer a flexible and efficient way to do this, providing a range of products tailored to different risk profiles, time horizons, and investment objectives.

Through this book, I've aimed to equip you with the knowledge and tools necessary to confidently navigate the often complex world of mutual funds. From the basics of how mutual funds work to the specifics of how NRIs can invest in them, we've walked through every step of the process to help you make informed decisions.

We've covered the regulatory frameworks, tax implications, and investment strategies that will allow you to build a portfolio that not only meets your financial goals but also mitigates risks along the way.

More importantly, this book emphasises that wealth creation through mutual funds is not a sprint but a marathon. Every step you take, whether it's setting up a Systematic Investment Plan (SIP), choosing the right sectoral funds, or maintaining a disciplined approach to your investments, is part of a larger journey towards financial freedom.

The beauty of mutual funds lies in their ability to compound returns over time, allowing even small, consistent investments to grow into substantial wealth. As we've seen through various case studies and examples, the key to success lies in persistence, patience, and a long-term outlook.

Taxation and regulations may initially seem like obstacles, but they are manageable challenges that can be effectively navigated with the right knowledge. Understanding the tax implications of your investments, especially as an NRI with potential tax liabilities in multiple countries, is crucial to maximising your returns.

The chapters on Double Taxation Avoidance Agreements (DTAAs) and SEBI regulations were included to help you minimise tax burdens and remain compliant with local laws, ensuring that you get to keep more of what you earn. While tax rules may evolve, staying informed and proactive about your tax strategy will protect your portfolio and ensure it grows steadily.

India's economy is evolving rapidly, with sectors like technology, renewable energy, and infrastructure presenting enormous growth opportunities. These emerging industries are not just the future of India, they are the future of global markets. As an NRI investor, you have the ability to tap into these high-growth sectors at the right time, positioning your portfolio for significant returns in the years to come.

Diversifying your investments to include these forward-looking sectors can help balance risk while capitalising on the vast potential of the Indian market. This foresight is what will allow you to not only create wealth but to preserve and grow it for future generations.

Speaking of future generations, one of the underlying themes of this book is the idea of leaving behind a financial legacy. Mutual fund investing allows you to grow wealth over time, but it also enables you to provide for your loved ones in a meaningful way.

The decisions you make today can impact your family for decades, ensuring that they have the financial stability and opportunities to thrive. Whether it's funding a child's education, providing for a comfortable retirement, or building a foundation for future investments, the wealth you accumulate through mutual funds can have lasting effects.

In addition, we've discussed how to structure your portfolio to ensure it remains robust and resilient through market cycles. We explored how to balance between equity and debt funds, how to assess your risk tolerance, and how to select funds that align with your financial goals.

These strategies, when executed consistently, can transform your investments from mere financial tools into a powerful vehicle for long-term wealth creation. It's not just about growing your personal wealth, it's about creating a financial ecosystem that can benefit your family, community, and future generations.

The flexibility that mutual funds offer makes them an ideal choice for NRIs who may have changing financial goals, geographical shifts, or varied risk appetites over time. Whether you are seeking aggressive growth in your younger years, looking to preserve capital as you near retirement, or planning to pass on a legacy to your heirs, mutual funds offer a solution that can be tailored to your needs at every stage of life.

Lastly, I want to remind you that wealth creation is not just about accumulating money, it's about achieving financial freedom and security. It's about giving yourself and your loved ones the freedom to pursue your passions, dreams, and goals without financial constraints. With a well-thought-out mutual fund investment strategy, you're not just building wealth for today; you're laying the foundation for a brighter, more secure future.

As you move forward, continue to educate yourself, remain patient, and keep your long-term vision in focus. Stay disciplined, review your portfolio periodically, and adjust your strategy as needed, always with your ultimate financial objectives in mind. Remember that every investment decision you make is a step toward creating wealth that can transcend borders, overcome challenges, and build a lasting legacy.

Here's to your continued success on this exciting journey of wealth creation, one that will endure for generations to come.

## Disclaimer

I am not a financial advisor: The information provided in this book is based solely on my personal experiences and opinions. It is not intended as financial advice. Before making any investment decisions, you should consult with a qualified financial advisor or accountant.

Jugal Kishore Baldawa and associated companies are not liable for any losses or damages arising from the use or reliance on the information provided in this book. The information is provided on an "as is" basis without any warranties, express or implied, including but not limited to warranties of merchantability, fitness for a particular purpose, or non-infringement.

You should always do your own due diligence before making any investment decisions. This includes researching the investment, understanding the risks involved, and considering your own financial situation and risk tolerance. Past performance is not indicative of future results, and there is no guarantee that any investment strategy will be successful.

Please note that this disclaimer is intended to provide general information and does not constitute legal advice. If you have specific legal questions, you should consult with an attorney.

www.ingramcontent.com/pod-product-compliance
Lightning Source LLC
Chambersburg PA
CBHW031442210526
45464CB00005B/2307